Spanish

phrase book & dictionary

Berlitz Publishing
New York   London   Singapore

Contacting the Editors
Every effort has been made to provide accurate information in this publication, but changes are inevitable. The publisher cannot be responsible for any resulting loss, inconvenience or injury. We would appreciate it if readers would call our attention to any errors or outdated information. We also welcome your suggestions; if you come across a relevant expression not in our phrase book, please contact us at: **comments@berlitzpublishing.com**

Twelfth Printing: April 2012
Printed in China

Publishing Director: Mina Patria
Commissioning Editor: Kate Drynan
Editorial Assistant: Sophie Cooper
Translation: updated by Wordbank
Cover Design: Beverley Speight
Interior Design: Beverley Speight
Production Manager: Raj Trivedi
Picture Researcher: Lucy Johnston
Cover Photo: Main 'market' photo, 'library' pic, 'flowerpot' photo Greg Gladman/APA; 'Dome ceiling' photo, 'tiles' photo, 'Gaudi' photo Gregory Wrona/APA; 'Currency' photo Lucy Johnston/APA.

Interior Photos: Neil Buchan-Grant/APA 111; Kevin Cummins/APA 38; Greg Gladman/APA 1, 12, 18, 57, 60, 100, 114, 169, iStockphoto 48, 117, 135, 149, 152; Britta Jaschinski/APA 16, 88, 92, 147, 157; Lucy Johnston/APA 15, 175; Sylvaine Poitau/APA 97; Gregory Wrona/APA 79, 101, 107, 132, 141.

Contents

Food & Drink

People

Leisure Time

Special Requirements

In an Emergency

Dictionary

Pronunciation

This section is designed to make you familiar with the sounds of Spanish using our simplified phonetic transcription. You'll find the pronunciation of the Spanish letters and sounds explained below, together with their 'imitated' equivalents. This system is used throughout the phrase book; simply read the pronunciation as if it were English, noting any special rules below.

Underlined letters indicate that that syllable should be stressed. The acute accent ´ indicates stress, e.g. **río**, _ree-oh_. Some Spanish words have more than one meaning. In these instances, the accent mark is also used to distinguish between them, e.g.: **él** (he) and **el** (the); **sí** (yes) and **si** (if).

There are some differences in vocabulary and pronunciation between the Spanish spoken in Spain and that in the Americas, although each is easily understood by the other. This phrase book and dictionary is specifically geared to travelers in Spain.

Consonants

Letter	Approximate Pronunciation	Symbol	Example	Pronunciation
b	1. as in English	**b**	**bueno**	_bweh•noh_
	2. between vowels as in English, but softer	**b**	**bebida**	beh•_bee_•dah
c	1. before e and i like th in thin	**th**	**centro**	_thehn_•troh
	2. otherwise like k in kit	**k**	**como**	_koh_•moh
ch	as in English	**ch**	**mucho**	_moo_•choh

Letter	Approximate Pronunciation	Symbol	Example	Pronunciation
d	1. as in English	d	**donde**	_dohn_•deh
	2. between vowels and especially at the end of a word, like th in thin, but softer	th	**usted**	oos•_teth_
g	1. before e and i, like ch in Scottish loch	kh	**urgente**	oor•_khehn_•teh
	2. otherwise, like g in get	g	**ninguno**	neen•_goo_•noh
h	always silent		**hombre**	_ohm_•breh
j	like ch in Scottish loch	kh	**bajo**	_bah_•khoh
ll	like y in yellow	y	**lleno**	_yeh_•noh
ñ	like ni in onion	ny	**señor**	seh•_nyohr_
q	like k in kick	k	**quince**	_keen_•theh
r	trilled, especially at the beginning of a word	r	**río**	_ree_•oh
rr	strongly trilled	rr	**arriba**	ah•_rree_•bah
s	1. like s in same	s	**sus**	soos
	2. before b, d, g, l, m, n, like s in rose	z	**mismo**	_meez_•moh
v	like b in bad, but softer	b	**viejo**	_beeyeh_•khoh
z	like th in thin	th	**brazo**	_brah_•thoh

Letters f, k, l, m, n, p, t, w, x and y are pronounced as in English.

Vowels

Letter	Approximate Pronunciation	Symbol	Example	Pronunciation
a	like the a in father	**ah**	**gracias**	_grah•theeyahs_
e	like e in get	**eh**	**esta**	_ehs•tah_
i	like ee in meet	**ee**	**sí**	_see_
o	like o in rope	**oh**	**dos**	_dohs_
u	1. like oo in food	**oo**	**uno**	_oo•noh_
	2. silent after g and q		**que**	_keh_
	3. when marked ü, like we in well	**w**	**antigüedad**	_ahn•tee•gweh•dahd_
y	1. like y in yellow	**y**	**hoy**	_oy_
	2. when alone, like ee in meet	**ee**	**y**	_ee_
	3. when preceded by an a, sounds like y + ee, with ee faintly pronounced	**aye**	**hay**	_aye_

With over 400 million Spanish speakers worldwide, Spanish is the third most widely spoken language in the world and the official language of 21 different nations. Over 17 million people in the United States speak Spanish as their native language, and it is one of the official languages of the United Nations. Spanish is the fourth most popular language on the internet, behind English, Japanese and German. Below are estimated numbers of Spanish speakers around the globe.

Central America: 55 million
North America: 112 million
South America: 190 million
Spain: 40 million

How to use this Book

Sometimes you see two alternatives separated by a slash. Choose the one that's right for your situation.

ESSENTIAL

I'm on vacation

Estoy aquí de vacaciones/en viaje de [holiday]/business. negocios. ehs·*toy* ah·*kee* deh bah·kah·*theeyohn*·ehs/ ehn *beeyah*·kheh deh neh·*goh*·theeyohs

I'm going to...
Voy a... boy ah...

I'm staying at the... Hotel.
Me alojo en el Hotel... meh ah·*loh*·khoh ehn ehl oh·*tehl*...

Words you may see are shown in YOU MAY SEE boxes.

YOU MAY SEE...

ADUANAS	customs
ARTÍCULOS LIBRES DE IMPUESTOS	duty-free goods
ARTÍCULOS QUE DECLARAR	goods to declare

Any of the words or phrases listed can be plugged into the sentence below.

Bicycle & Motorcycle

I'd like to rent [hire]...
Quiero alquilar... *keeyeh*·roh ahl·kee·*lahr*...

  a bicycle
    una bicicleta *oo*·nah bee·thee·*kleh*·tah

  a moped
    un ciclomotor oon thee·kloh·moh·*tohr*

  a motorcycle
    una motocicleta *oo*·nah moh·toh·thee·*kleh*·tah

How much per day/week?
¿Cuánto cuesta por día/semana? *kwahn*·toh *kwehs*·tah pohr *dee*·ah/seh·*mah*·nah

Spanish phrases appear in purple.

Read the simplified pronunciation as if it were English. For more on pronunciation, see page 7.

The Dating Game

Can I join you?

¿Puedo acompañarle *m*/acompañarla *f*?
*pweh•doh ah•kohm•pah•nyahr•leh **m**/ ah•kohm•pah•nyahr•lah **f***

You're very attractive.
For Grammar, see page 162.

Eres muy guapo *m*/guapa *f*.
*eh•rehs mooy gwah•poh **m**/gwah•pah **f***

Related phrases can be found by going to the page number indicated.

When different gender forms apply, the masculine form is followed by *m*; feminine by *f*

When addressing strangers, always use the more formal **usted** (singular) or **ustedes** (plural), as opposed to the more familiar **tú** (singular) or **vosotros** (plural), until told otherwise. If you know someone's title, it's polite to use it, e.g., **doctor** (male doctor), **doctora** (female doctor). You can also simply say **Señor** (Mr.), **Señora** (Mrs.) or **Señorita** (Miss).

Information boxes contain relevant country, culture and language tips.

Expressions you may hear are shown in You May Hear boxes.

YOU MAY HEAR...

Hablo muy poco inglés.   I only speak a little English.
ah•bloh mooy poh•koh een•glehs

Color-coded side bars identify each section of the book.

Survival

Arrival & Departure

ESSENTIAL

I'm on vacation/ business.	**Estoy aquí de vacaciones/en viaje de negocios.** *ehs·toy ah·kee deh bah·kah·theeyohn·ehs/ ehn beeyah·kheh deh neh·goh·theeyohs*
I'm going to...	**Voy a...** *boy ah...*
I'm staying at the... Hotel.	**Me alojo en el Hotel...** *meh ah·loh·khoh ehn ehl oh·tehl...*

YOU MAY HEAR...

Su pasaporte, por favor.
soo pah·sah·pohr·teh pohr fah·bohr

Your passport, please.

¿Cuál es el propósito de su visita?
kwahl ehs ehl proh·poh·see·toh deh soo bee·see·tah

What's the purpose of your visit?

¿Dónde se aloja?
dohn·deh seh ah·loh·khah

Where are you staying?

¿Cuánto tiempo piensa quedarse?
kwahn·toh teeyehm·poh peeyehn·sah keh·dar·seh

How long are you staying?

¿Con quién viaja?
kohn keeyehn beeyah·khah

Who are you here with?

Border Control

I'm just passing through.	**Estoy de paso.** ehs·_toy_ deh _pah_·soh
I'd like to declare…	**Quiero declarar…** _keeyeh_·roh deh·klah·_rahr_…
I have nothing to declare.	**No tengo nada que declarar.** noh _tehn_·goh _nah_·dah keh deh·klah·_rahr_

YOU MAY HEAR…

¿Tiene algo que declarar?
teeyeh·neh _ahl_·goh keh deh·klah·_rahr_

Anything to declare?

Tiene que pagar impuestos por esto.
teeyeh·neh keh pah·_gahr_ eem·_pwehs_·tohs pohr _ehs_·toh

You must pay duty on this.

Abra esta maleta.
_ah_·brah _ehs_·tah mah·_leh_·tah

Open this bag.

YOU MAY SEE…

ADUANAS	customs
ARTÍCULOS LIBRES DE IMPUESTOS	duty-free goods
ARTÍCULOS QUE DECLARAR	goods to declare
NADA QUE DECLARAR	nothing to declare
CONTROL DE PASAPORTES	passport control
POLICÍA	police

Money

ESSENTIAL

Where's...?	**¿Dónde está...?** _dohn_•deh ehs•_tah_...
the ATM	**el cajero automático** _ehl kah_•_kheh_•roh _awtoh_•_mah_•tee•koh
the bank	**el banco** _ehl bahn_•koh
the currency exchange office	**la casa de cambio** _lah kah_•sah deh _kahm_•beeyoh
When does the bank open/close?	**¿A qué hora abre/cierra el banco?** _ah keh oh_•rah _ah_•breh/_theeyeh_•rrah ehl _bahn_•koh
I'd like to change dollars/pounds into euros.	**Quiero cambiar dólares/libras a euros.** _keeyeh_•roh kahm•_beeyahr doh_•lah•rehs/_lee_•brahs ah _ew_•rohs
I'd like to cash traveler's checks [cheques].	**Quiero cobrar cheques de viaje.** _keeyeh_•roh koh•_brahr cheh_•kehs deh _beeyah_•kheh

YOU MAY SEE…

INTRODUCIR TARJETA AQUÍ	insert card here
CANCELAR	cancel
BORRAR	clear
INTRODUCIR	enter
CLAVE	PIN
RETIRAR FONDOS	withdraw funds
DE CUENTA CORRIENTE	from checking [current] account
DE CUENTA DE AHORROS	from savings account
RECIBO	receipt

At the Bank

I'd like to change money/get a cash advance.
Quiero cambiar dinero/un adelanto de efectivo.
keeyeh•roh kahm•beeyahr dee•neh•roh/
oon ah•deh•lahn•toh deh eh•fehk•tee•boh

What's the exchange rate?
¿Cuál es el tipo de cambio? _kwahl ehs ehl_
tee•poh deh kahm•beeyoh

How much is the fee? **¿Cuánto es la tasa?** _kwahn•toh ehs lah tah•sah_

I lost my traveler's checks.
He perdido los cheques de viaje.
eh pehr•dee•doh lohs cheh•kehs deh beeyah•kheh

My card was lost.	**Se me ha perdido la tarjeta.**
	seh meh ah pehr·dee·doh lah tahr·kheh·tah
My card was stolen.	**Me han robado la tarjeta.**
	meh ahn roh·bah·doh lah tahr·kheh·tah
My card doesn't work.	**Mi tarjeta no funciona.** *mee tahr·kheh·tah noh foon·theeyoh·nah*
The ATM ate my card.	**El cajero automático se ha tragado mi tarjeta.**
	ehl kah·kheh·roh awtoh·mah·tee·koh seh ah trah·gah·doh mee tahr·kheh·tah

For Numbers, see page 167.

ATMs are located throughout Spain. Cash can be obtained from ATMs with Visa™, Eurocard™, American Express® and many other international cards. Instructions are often given in English. Debit cards are becoming a more accepted method of payment in Spain. Whether using a credit card or debit card, make sure you have your PIN (personal identification number) and that it is four digits. If you have an alphabetic PIN, be aware that Spanish ATMs do not have letters on the keypad. The best rates for exchanging money will be found at banks and ATMs. You can change money at travel agencies and hotels, but the rate will not be as good. Remember your passport when you want to change money.

YOU MAY SEE...

Spanish currency is the **euro**, **€**, divided into 100 **céntimos** (cents).
Coins: 1, 2, 5, 10, 20, 50 **cts**.; **€**1, 2
Notes: **€**5, 10, 20, 50, 100, 200, 500

Getting Around

ESSENTIAL

How do I get to town?	**¿Cómo se llega a la ciudad?** _koh•moh seh yeh•gah ah lah theew•dahd_
Where's…?	**¿Dónde está…?** _dohn•deh ehs•tah…_
the airport	**el aeropuerto** _ehl ah•eh•roh•pwehr•toh_
the train [railway] station	**la estación de tren** _lah ehs•tah•theeyohn deh trehn_
the bus station	**la estación de autobuses** _lah ehs•tah•theeyohn deh awtoh•booses_
the metro station	**la estación de metro** _lah ehs•tah•theeyohn deh meh•troh_
Is it far from here?	**¿A qué distancia está?** _ah keh dees•tahn•theeyah ehs•tah_
Where do I buy a ticket?	**¿Dónde se compra el billete?** _dohn•deh seh kohm•prah ehl bee•yeh•teh_
A one-way/return-trip ticket to…	**Un billete de ida/ida y vuelta a…** _oon bee•yeh•teh deh ee•dah/ee•dah ee bwehl•tah ah…_

How much?	**¿Cuánto es?** _kwahn_·toh ehs
Is there a discount?	**¿Hacen descuento?** _ah_·then dehs·_kwehn_·toh
Which...?	**¿De qué...?** deh keh...
gate	**puerta de embarque** _pwehr_·tah deh ehm·_bahr_·keh
line	**línea** _lee_·neh·ah
platform	**andén** ahn·_dehn_
Where can I get a taxi?	**¿Dónde puedo coger un taxi?** _dohn_·deh _pweh_·doh koh·_khehr_ oon _tah_·xee
Take me to this address.	**Lléveme a esta dirección.** _yeh_·beh·meh ah _ehs_·tah dee·rek·_theeyohn_
Where's the car hire?	**¿Dónde está el alquiler de coches?** _dohn_·deh ehs·_tah_ ehl ahl·kee·_lehr_ deh _koh_·chehs
Can I have a map?	**¿Podría darme un mapa?** poh·_dree_·ah _dahr_·meh oon _mah_·pah

Tickets

When's...to Madrid?	**¿Cuándo sale...a Madrid?** _kwahn_·doh _sah_·leh...ah mah·_dreeth_
the (first) bus	**el (primer) autobús** ehl (pree·_mehr_) awtoh·_boos_
the (next) flight	**el (próximo) vuelo** ehl (_proh_·xee·moh) _bweh_·loh
the (last) train	**el (último) tren** ehl (_ool_·tee·moh) trehn
Where do I buy a ticket?	**¿Dónde se compra el billete?** _dohn_·deh seh _kohm_·prah ehl bee·_yeh_·teh
One/Two ticket(s), please.	**Un/Dos billete(s), por favor.** oon/dohs bee·_yeh_·teh(s) pohr fah·_bohr_
For today/tomorrow.	**Para hoy/mañana.** _pah_·rah oy/mah·_nyah_·nah
A...ticket.	**Un billete...** oon bee·_yeh_·teh...
one-way	**de ida** deh _ee_·dah
return-trip	**de ida y vuelta** deh _ee_·dah ee _bwehl_·tah
first class	**de primera clase** deh pree·_meh_·rah _klah_·she

business class	**de clase preferente** deh _klah_·seh preh·feh·_rehn_·teh
economy class	**de clase económica** deh _klah_·seh eh·koh·_noh_·mee·kah
How much?	**¿Cuánto es?** _kwahn_·toh ehs
Is there a discount for…?	**¿Hacen descuento a…?** _ah_·thehn dehs·_kwehn_·toh ah…
children	**los niños** lohs _nee_·nyohs
students	**los estudiantes** lohs ehs·too·_deeyahn_·tehs
senior citizens	**los jubilados** lohs khoo·bee·_lah_·dohs
tourists	**los turistas** too·_rees_·tahs

The express bus/express train, please.	**El autobús exprés/tren exprés, por favor.** ehl awtoh·boos/trehn ex·presh, pohr fah·bohr
The local bus/train, please.	**El autobús/tren local, por favor.** ehl awtoh·boos/trehn loh·kahl, pohr fah·bohr
I have an e-ticket.	**Tengo un billete electrónico.** _tehn_·goh oon bee·_yeh_·teh eh·lehk·_troh_·nee·koh
Can I buy a ticket on the bus/train?	**¿Puedo comprar el billete a bordo del autobús/tren?** _pweh_·doh kohm·_prahr_ ehl bee·_yeh_·teh ah _bohr_·doh dehl awtoh·_boos_/trehn
Do I have to stamp the ticket before boarding?	**¿Tengo que sellar el billete antes de embarcar?** _tehn_·goh keh seh·yahr ehl bee·yeh·teh ahn·tehs deh ehm·bahr·kahr
How long is this ticket valid?	**¿Cuál es la validez de este billete?** kwahl ehs lah bah·lee·dehth deh ehs·teh bee·yeh·teh
Can I return on the same ticket?	**¿Puedo volver con el mismo billete?** pweh·doh bohl·behr kohn ehl meesh·moh bee·yeh·teh
I'd like to…my reservation.	**Quiero…mi reserva.** _keeyeh_·roh…mee reh·_sehr_·bah
cancel	**cancelar** kahn·theh·_lahr_
change	**cambiar** kahm·_beeyahr_
confirm	**confirmar** kohn·feer·_mahr_

For Time, see page 170.

Plane

Airport Transfer

How much is a taxi to the airport?	**¿Cuánto cuesta el trayecto en taxi al aeropuerto?** _kwahn•toh kwehs•tah ehl trah•yehk•toh ehn tah•xee ahl ah•eh•roh•pwehr•toh_
To…Airport, please.	**Al aeropuerto de…, por favor.** _ahl ah•eh•roh•pwehr•toh deh…pohr fah•bohr_
My airline is…	**Mi compañía aérea es…** _mee kohm•pah•nyee•ah ah•eh•reh•ah ehs…_
My flight leaves at…	**Mi vuelo sale a la/las…** _mee bweh•loh sah•leh ah lah/lahs…_
I'm in a rush.	**Tengo prisa.** _tehn•goh pree•sah_
Can you take an alternate route?	**¿Puede coger otro camino?** _pweh•deh koh•khehr oh•troh kah•mee•noh_
Can you drive faster/slower?	**¿Puede ir más deprisa/despacio?** _pweh•deh eer mahs deh•pree•sah/dehs•pah•theeyoh_

For Grammar, see page 162.

For Time, see page 170.

YOU MAY HEAR…

¿Con qué compañía aérea viaja?
kohn keh kohm•pah•nyee•ah ah•eh•reh•ah beeyah•khah

What airline are you flying?

¿Nacional o internacional?
nah•theeyoh•nahl oh een•tehr•nah•theeyoh•nahl

Domestic or international?

¿Qué terminal? _keh tehr•mee•nahl_

What terminal?

YOU MAY SEE...

LLEGADAS	arrivals
SALIDAS	departures
RECOGIDA DE EQUIPAJES	baggage claim
VUELOS NACIONALES	domestic flights
VUELOS INTERNACIONALES	international flights
MOSTRADOR DE FACTURACIÓN	check-in
FACTURACIÓN ELECTRÓNICA	e-ticket check-in
PUERTAS DE EMBARQUE	departure gates

Checking In

Where's check-in?	**¿Dónde está el mostrador de facturación?** _dohn·deh ehs·tah ehl mohs·trah·dohr deh fahk·too·rah·theeyohn_
My name is...	**Me llamo...** _meh yah·moh..._
I'm going to...	**Voy a...** _boy ah..._
I have...	**Tengo...** _tehn·goh_
one suitcase	**una maleta** _oo·nah mah·leh·tah_
two suitcases	**dos maletas** _dohs mah·leh·tahs_
one piece of hand luggage	**una pieza de equipaje de mano** _oo·nah peeyeh·thah deh eh·kee·pah·kheh deh mah·noh_
How much luggage is allowed?	**¿Cuánto equipaje está permitido?** _kwahn·toh eh·kee·pah·kheh ehs·tah pehr·mee·tee·doh_
Is that pounds or kilos?	**¿Son libras o kilos?** _sohn lee·brahs oh kee·lohs_
Which terminal/gate?	**¿De qué terminal/puerta de embarque?** _deh keh tehr·mee·nahl/pwehr·tah deh ehm·bahr·keh_
I'd like a window/an aisle seat.	**Quiero un asiento de ventana/pasillo.** _keeyeh·roh oon ah·seeyehn·toh deh behn·tah·nah/pah·see·yoh_

When do we leave/arrive?	**¿A qué hora salimos/llegamos?** *ah keh oh•rah sah•lee•mohs/yeh•gah•mohs*
Is the flight delayed?	**¿Lleva retraso el vuelo?** *yeh•bah reh•trah•soh ehl bweh•loh*
How late?	**¿Cuánto retraso lleva?** *kwahn•toh reh•trah•soh yeh•bah*

YOU MAY HEAR...

¡Siguiente! *see•geeyehn•teh* — Next!

Su pasaporte/billete, por favor. *soo pah•sah•pohr•teh/bee•yeh•teh pohr fah•bohr* — Your passport/ticket, please.

¿Va a facturar el equipaje? *bah ah fahk•too•rahr ehl eh•kee•pah•kheh* — Are you checking in any luggage?

Lleva exceso de equipaje. *yeh•bah ehx•theh•soh deh eh•kee•pah•kheh* — You have excess luggage.

Eso es demasiado grande para equipaje de mano. *eh•soh ehs deh•mah•seeyah•doh grahn•deh pah•rah eh•kee•pah•kheh deh mah•noh* — That's too large for a carry-on [to carry on board].

¿Hizo las maletas usted? *ee•thoh lahs mah•leh•tahs oos•teth* — Did you pack these bags yourself?

¿Le entregó alguien algún paquete? *leh ehn•treh•goh ahl•geeyehn ahl•goon pah•keh•teh* — Did anyone give you anything to carry?

Vacíese los bolsillos. *bah•thee•eh•seh lohs bohl•see•yohs* — Empty your pockets.

Quítese los zapatos. *kee•teh•seh lohs thah•pah•tohs* — Take off your shoes.

Se está efectuando el embarque del vuelo... *seh ehs•tah eh•fehk•too•ahn•doh ehl ehm•bahr•keh dehl bweh•loh...* — Now boarding flight...

Luggage

Where is/are...?	**¿Dónde está/están...?** <u>dohn</u>·deh ehs·<u>tah</u>/ ehs·<u>tahn</u>...
the luggage carts [trolleys]	**los carritos para el equipaje** lohs kah·<u>rree</u>·tohs <u>pah</u>·rah ehl eh·kee·<u>pah</u>·kheh
the luggage lockers	**las consignas automáticas** lahs kohn·<u>seeg</u>·nahs awtoh·<u>mah</u>·tee·kahs
the baggage claim	**la recogida de equipajes** lah reh·koh·<u>khee</u>·dah deh eh·kee·<u>pah</u>·k hehs
My luggage has been lost.	**Han perdido mi equipaje.** ahn pehr·<u>dee</u>·doh mee eh·kee·<u>pah</u>·kheh
My luggage has been stolen.	**Me han robado el equipaje.** meh ahn roh·<u>bah</u>·doh ehl eh·kee·<u>pah</u>·kheh
My suitcase is damaged.	**Mi maleta ha sufrido daños.** mee mah·<u>leh</u>·tah ah soo·<u>free</u>·doh <u>dah</u>·nyohs

Finding your Way

Where is/are...?	**¿Dónde está/están...?** <u>dohn</u>·deh ehs·<u>tah</u>/ehs·<u>tahn</u>...
the currency exchange	**la casa de cambio** lah <u>kah</u>·sah deh <u>kahm</u>·beeyoh
the car hire	**el alquiler de coches** ehl ahl·kee·<u>lehr</u> deh <u>koh</u>·chehs
the exit	**la salida** lah sah·<u>lee</u>·dah
the taxis	**los taxis** lohs <u>tah</u>·xees
Is there...into town?	**¿Hay...que vaya a la ciudad?** aye... keh <u>bah</u>·yah ah lah theew·<u>dahd</u>
a bus	**un autobús** on awtoh·<u>boos</u>
a train	**un tren** on trehn
a metro	**un metro** on <u>meh</u>·troh

For Asking Directions, see page 34.

Train

Where's the train station?	**¿Dónde está la estación de tren?** *dohn•deh ehs•tah lah ehs•tah•theeyohn deh trehn*
How far is it?	**¿A qué distancia está?** *ah keh dees•tahn•theeyah ehs•tah*
Where is/are…?	**¿Dónde está/están…?** *dohn•deh ehs•tah/ehs•tahn…*
the ticket office	**el despacho de billetes** *ehl dehs•pah•choh deh bee•yeh•tehs*
the information desk	**el mostrador de información** *ehl mohs•trah•dohr deh een•fohr•mah•theeyohn*
the luggage lockers	**las consignas automáticas** *lahs kohn•seeg•nahs awtoh•mah•tee•kahs*
the platforms	**los andenes** *lohs ahn•deh•nehs*
Can I have a schedule [timetable]?	**¿Podría darme un horario?** *poh•dree•ah dahr•meh oon oh•rah•reeyoh*
How long is the trip?	**¿Cuánto dura el viaje?** *kwahn•toh doo•rah ehl veeyah•kheh*
Is it a direct train?	**¿Es un tren directo?** *ehs oon trehn dee•rehk•toh*
Do I have to change trains?	**¿Tengo que cambiar de trenes?** *tehn•goh keh kahm•beeyahr deh treh•nehs*
Is the train on time?	**¿El tren va puntual?** *ehl trehn bah poon•tooahl*

For Asking Directions, see page 34.

YOU MAY SEE…

ANDENES	platforms
INFORMACIÓN	information
RESERVAS	reservations
SALA DE ESPERA	waiting room
LLEGADAS	arrivals
SALIDAS	departures

Spain's major railway network is **RENFE**, **Red Nacional de Ferrocarriles Españoles**. RENFE offers a variety of train types, from express to local, national to international. You can purchase tickets or make reservations through the **RENFE** website or a travel agency, or at the station. It is sometimes necessary to purchase your tickets a day or two in advance for popular routes.

Departures

Which track [platform] for the train to…?	**¿De qué andén sale el tren a…?** *deh keh ahn-dehn sah-leh ehl trehn ah…*
Is this the track [platform]/train to…?	**¿Es éste el andén/tren a…?** *ehs ehs-teh ehl ahn-dehn/trehn ah…*
Where is track [platform]…?	**¿Dónde está el andén…?** *dohn-deh ehs-tah ehl ahn-dehn…*
Where do I change for…?	**¿Dónde tengo que cambiar para…?** *dohn-deh tehn-goh keh kahm-beeyahr pah-rah…*

YOU MAY HEAR…

¡Todos a bordo! *toh-dohs ah bohr-doh*	All aboard!
Billetes, por favor. *bee-yeh-tehs pohr fah-bohr*	Tickets, please.
Tiene que cambiar de tren en León. *teeyeh-neh keh kahm-beeyahr deh trehn ehn leh-ohn*	You have to change at Léon.
Próxima parada: Madrid. *proh-xee-mah pah-rah-dah mah-dreeth*	Next stop, Madrid.

On Board

Can I sit here?	**¿Le importa si me siento aquí?** *leh eem·pohr·tah see meh seeyehn·toh ah·kee*
Can I open the window?	**Puedo abrir la ventana?** *pweh·doh ah·breer lah behn·tah·nah*
That's my seat.	**Ése es mi asiento.** *eh·seh ehs mee ah·seeyehn·toh*
Here's my reservation.	**Esta es mi reserva.** *ehs·tah ehs mee reh·sehr·bah*

Bus

Where's the bus station?	**¿Dónde está la estación de autobuses?** *dohn·deh ehs·tah lah ehs·tah·theeyohn deh awtoh·boo·sehs*
How far is it?	**¿A qué distancia está?** *ah keh dees·tahn·theeyah ehs·tah*
How do I get to…?	**¿Cómo se llega a…?** *koh·moh seh yeh·gah ah…*
Is this the bus to…?	**¿Es éste el autobús a…?** *ehs ehs·teh ehl awtoh·boos ah…*
How many stops to…?	**¿Cuántas paradas hay hasta…?** *kwahn·tahs pah·rah·dahs aye ahs·tah…*

Bus service in Spain is extensive. For local service within a town, you usually pay as you board the bus. The fare is generally a fixed price. In larger cities, bus tickets are interchangeable with subway tickets. **Un bono** (**metrobús** in Madrid), a ten-trip ticket, is the cheapest way to go. These tickets are available at newsstands, banks, lottery-ticket shops and subway stations. When using the **bono** on a bus, make sure to validate your ticket by stamping it in the machine next to the driver as you board. Signal that you wish to get off by pushing a button, located throughout the bus; a sign will light up that says **parada solicitada** (stop requested).

YOU MAY SEE...

PARADA DE AUTOBUSES	bus stop
SUBIR/BAJAR	enter/exit
PICAR BILLETE	stamp your ticket

Can you tell me when to get off?	**¿Podría decirme cuándo me tengo que bajar?** *poh·dree·ah deh·theer·meh kwahn·doh meh tehn·goh keh bah·khahr*
Do I have to change buses?	**¿Tengo que hacer transbordo?** *tehn·goh keh ah·thehr trahns·bohr·doh*
Stop here, please!	**¡Pare aquí, por favor!** *pah·reh ah·kee pohr fah·bohr*

For Tickets, see page 19.

Metro

Where's the metro?	**¿Dónde está la estación de metro?** *dohn·deh ehs·tah lah ehs·tah·theeyohn deh meh·troh*
A map, please.	**Un plano, por favor.** *oon plah·noh pohr fah·bohr*

In Spain, there are **metro** (subway) systems in Madrid, Barcelona, Valencia and Bilbao. **Metro** systems are easy to use and reasonably priced. All three **metro** systems operate on a one-way, per-ride basis. You can save money by buying a 10-trip ticket or **un bono** (**metrobús** in Madrid), which can be purchased at **metro** stations, banks, newsstands and tobacco shops. In larger cities, **metro** and bus tickets are the same price and are interchangeable.
To enter the subway system, slip your ticket through the slot in the turnstile; remember to grab your ticket, which now has the date printed on it, so that you can pass through the turnstile.

Which line for…?	**¿Qué línea tengo que coger para…?** *keh lee-neh-ah tehn-goh keh koh-khehr pah-rah…*
Which direction?	**¿Qué dirección?** *keh dee-rehk-theeyohn*
Do I have to transfer [change]?	**¿Tengo que hacer transbordo?** *tehn-goh keh ah-thehr trahns-bohr-doh*
Is this the metro [train] to…?	**¿Es éste el tren a…?** *ehs ehs-teh ehl trehn ah…*
How many stops to…?	**¿Cuántas paradas hay hasta…?** *kwahn-tahs pah-rah-dahs aye ahs-tah*
Where are we?	**¿Dónde estamos?** *dohn-deh ehs-tah-mohs*

For Tickets, see page 19.

Boat & Ferry

When is the ferry to…?	**¿Cuándo sale el ferry a…?** *kwahn-doh sah-leh ehl feh-rree ah…*
Can I take my car?	**¿Puedo llevar el coche?** *pweh-doh yeh-bahr ehl koh-cheh*
What time is the next sailing?	**¿A qué hora sale el siguiente barco?** *ah keh oh-rah sah-leh ehl see-geeyehn-teh bahr-koh*
Can I book a seat/cabin?	**¿Puedo reservar un asiento/camarote?** *pweh-doh reh-sehr-bahr oon ah-seeyehn-toh/kah-mah-roh-teh*
How long is the crossing?	**¿Cuánto dura la travesía?** *kwahn-toh doo-rah lah trah-beh-see-ah*

For Tickets, see page 19.

YOU MAY SEE…

| **BALSA SALVAVIDAS** | life boat |
| **CHALECO SALVAVIDAS** | life jacket |

In Spain, ferry and boat services run to and from the Balearic Islands (Mallorca, Menorca, Ibiza and Formentera), destinations in North Africa and the Canary Islands and ports in Genoa, Italy (from Barcelona) and southern England (from Bilbao and Santander).

Taxi

Where can I get a taxi?	**¿Dónde puedo coger un taxi?** <u>dohn</u>•deh <u>pweh</u>•doh koh•<u>khehr</u> oon tah•xee
Can you send a taxi?	**¿Puede enviar un taxi?** pweh•deh ehn•beeyahr oon tah•xee
Do you have the number for a taxi?	**¿Tiene el número de alguna empresa de taxi?** teeyeh•neh ehl <u>noo</u>•meh•roh deh ahl•<u>goo</u>•nah ehm•<u>preh</u>•sah deh <u>tah</u>•xee
I'd like a taxi now/ for tomorrow at…	**Quiero un taxi ahora/para mañana a la(s)…** <u>keeyeh</u>•roh oon <u>tah</u>•xee ah•<u>oh</u>•rah/<u>pah</u>•rah mah•<u>nyah</u>•nah ah lah(s)…
Pick me up at (place/time)…	**Recójame en/a la(s)…** reh•<u>koh</u>•khah•meh ehn/ah lah(s)…
I'm going to…	**Voy…** boy…
this address	**a esta dirección** ah <u>ehs</u>•tah dee•rehk•<u>theeyohn</u>
the airport	**al aeropuerto** ahl ah•eh•roh•<u>pwehr</u>•toh

In Spain, **coger** means to catch or get, as in: **¿Dónde puedo coger un taxi?** (Where can I catch a cab?). However, in Latin America, **coger** is a vulgarity for 'to have sex'. Use **tomar** (**¿Dónde puedo tomar un taxi?**) in Spanish-speaking Latin America.

YOU MAY HEAR...

¿Adónde se dirige? *ah-dohn-deh seh dee-ree-kheh*   Where to?

¿Cuál es la dirección? *kwahl ehs lah dee-rehk-theeyohn*   What's the address?

the train station	**a la estación de trenes** *ah lah ehs-tah-theeyohn deh treh-nehs*
I'm late.	**Llego tarde.** *yeh-goh tahr-deh*
Can you drive faster/slower?	**¿Puede ir más deprisa/despacio?** *pweh-deh eer mahs deh-pree-sah/dehs-pah-theeyoh*
Stop/Wait here.	**Pare/Espere aquí.** *pah-reh/ehs-peh-reh ah-kee*
How much?	**¿Cuánto es?** *kwahn-toh ehs*
You said it would cost...	**Dijo que costaría...** *dee-khoh keh kohs-tah-ree-ah...*
Keep the change.	**Quédese con el cambio.** *keh-deh-seh kohn ehl kahm-beeyoh*
A receipt, please.	**Un recibo, por favor.** *oon reh-thee-boh pohr fah-bohr*

For Grammar, see page 162.

In major Spanish cities, taxis are reasonably priced. Extra fees are usually charged for trips to the airport, bus station and train station and also for extra luggage. When entering the taxi, make sure the meter is turned on; it should register a base fare when the trip begins. The fare is then increased by a set amount per kilometer traveled.

Bicycle & Motorbike

I'd like to hire...	**Quiero alquilar...** _keeyeh_·roh ahl·kee·_lahr_...
a bicycle	**una bicicleta** _oo_·nah bee·thee·_kleh_·tah
a moped	**un ciclomotor** oon thee·kloh·moh·_tohr_
a motorcycle	**una motocicleta** _oo_·nah moh·toh·thee·_kleh_·tah
How much per day/week?	**¿Cuánto cuesta por día/semana?** _kwahn_·toh _kwehs_·tah pohr _dee_·ah/seh·_mah_·nah
Can I have a helmet/lock?	**¿Puede darme un casco/candado?** _pweh_·deh _dahr_·meh oon _kahs_·koh/kahn·_dah_·doh

Car Hire

Where's the car hire?	**¿Dónde está el alquiler de coches?** _dohn_·deh ehs·_tah_ ehl ahl·kee·_lehr_ deh _koh_·chehs
I'd like...	**Quiero...** _keeyeh_·roh...
a cheap/small car	**un coche económico/pequeño** oon _koh_·cheh eh·koh·_noh_·mee·koh/peh·_keh_·nyoh
an automatic/ a manual	**un coche automático/con transmisión manual** oon _koh_·cheh awtoh·_mah_·tee·koh/ kohn trahns·mee·_seeyohn_ mah·noo·_ahl_
air conditioning	**un coche con aire acondicionado** oon _koh_·cheh kohn _ayee_·reh ah·kohn·dee·theeyoh·_nah_·doh
a car seat	**un asiento de niño** oon ah·_seeyehn_·toh deh _nee_·nyoh
How much...?	**¿Cuánto cobran...?** _kwahn_·toh _koh_·brahn...
per day/week	**por día/semana** pohr _dee_·ah/seh·_mah_·nah
for...days	**por...días** pohr... _dee_·ahs
per kilometer	**por kilómetro** pohr kee·_loh_·meh·troh
for unlimited mileage	**por kilometraje ilimitado** pohr kee·loh·meh·_trah_·kheh ee·lee·mee·_tah_·doh
with insurance	**con el seguro** kohn ehl seh·_goo_·roh
Are there any discounts?	**¿Ofrecen algún descuento?** oh·_freh_·thehn ahl·_goon_ dehs·_kwehn_·toh

YOU MAY HEAR...

¿Tiene permiso de conducir internacional? _teeyeh•neh pehr•mee•soh deh kohn•doo•theer een•tehr•nah•theeyoh•nahl_
Do you have an international driver's license?

Su pasaporte, por favor.
soo pah•sah•pohr•teh pohr fah•bohr
Your passport, please.

¿Quiere seguro?
keeyeh•reh seh•goo•roh
Do you want insurance?

Tiene que dejar una fianza.
teeyeh•neh keh deh•khahr oo•nah fee•ahn•thah
I'll need a deposit.

Firme aquí. _feer•meh ah•kee_
Sign here.

Fuel Station

Where's the fuel station?	**¿Dónde está la gasolinera?** _dohn•deh ehs•tah lah gah•soh•lee•neh•rah_
Fill it up.	**Lleno.** _yeh•noh_
. . . liters, please.	**. . . litros, por favor.** . . . _lee•trohs pohr fah•bohr_
. . . euros, please.	**Euros por favor** _ew•rohs pohr fah-bohr_
I'll pay in cash/by credit card.	**Voy a pagar en efectivo/con tarjeta de crédito.** _boy ah pah•gahr ehn eh•fehk•tee•boh/ kohn tahr•kheh•tah deh kreh•dee•toh_

YOU MAY SEE...

NORMAL	regular
SÚPER	super
DIESEL	diesel

Asking Directions

Is this the way to…?	**¿Es ésta la carretera a…?** *ehs ehs·tah lah kah·rreh·teh·rah ah…*
How far is it to…?	**¿A qué distancia está…?** *ah keh dees·tahn·theeyah ehs·tah…*
Where's…?	**¿Dónde está…?** *dohn·deh ehs·tah…*
…Street	**la calle…** *lah kah·yeh…*
this address	**ésta dirección** *ehs·tah dee·rek·theeyohn*
the highway [motorway]	**la autopista** *lah aw·toh·pees·tah*
Can you show me on the map?	**¿Me lo puede indicar en el mapa?** *meh loh pweh·deh een·dee·kahr ehn ehl mah·pah*
I'm lost.	**Me he perdido.** *meh eh pehr·dee·doh*

YOU MAY HEAR…

todo recto *toh·doh rehk·toh*	straight ahead
a la izquierda *ah lah eeth·keeyehr·dah*	left
a la derecha *ah lah deh·reh·chah*	right
en/doblando la esquina *ehn/doh·blahn·doh lah ehs·kee·nah*	on/around the corner
frente a *frehn·teh ah*	opposite
detrás de *deh·trahs deh*	behind
al lado de *ahl lah·doh deh*	next to
después de *dehs·pwehs deh*	after
al norte/sur *ahl nohr·teh/soor*	north/south
al este/oeste *ahl ehs·teh/oh·ehs·teh*	east/west
en el semáforo *en ehl seh·mah·foh·roh*	at the traffic light
en el cruce *en ehl kroo·theh*	at the intersection

YOU MAY SEE...

	ADELANTAMIENTO PROHIBIDO	no passing zone
STOP	**STOP**	stop
	CALLE DE SENTIDO ÚNICO	one-way street
	CEDA EL PASO	yield [give way]
	ENTRADA PROHIBIDA	no entry
	ESTACIONAMIENTO PROHIBIDO	no parking
	FINAL DEL CARRIL LATERAL DERECHO	right lane ends (merge left)
50	**PROHIBICIÓN VELOCIDAD MÁXIMA**	maximum speed limit

Parking

Can I park here?	**¿Puedo aparcar aquí?** _pweh·doh ah·pahr·kahr ah·kee_
Where's...?	**¿Dónde está** _dohn·deh ehs·tah_
the parking garage/	**el garaje/aparcamiento?** _ehl gah·rah·kheh/_
parking lot?	_ah·pahr·kah·meeyehn·toh_
the parking meter?	**el parquímetro?** _ehl pahr·kee·meh·troh_
How much...?	**¿Cuánto cobran...?** _kwahn·toh koh·brahn..._
per hour	**por hora** _pohr oh·rah_
per day	**por día** _pohr dee·ah_
for overnight	**por la noche** _pohr lah noh·cheh_

Public parking is noted by a blue sign with a capital 'P'. Many towns have **zonas azules** (blue zones), where parking is allowed; buy a ticket at the nearby parking machine. Larger cities have an **ora zona** (hourly parking). Purchase a ticket for 30, 60 or 90 minutes and display it in your windshield. Tickets for the **ora zona** can be purchased at tobacconists, hotels and other retailers — look for the **ora zona** signs in the window. Note: Spain's **Guardia Civil de Tráfico** (highway patrol) may enforce payment of fines for illegal parking on the spot for non-residents of Spain.

Breakdown & Repair

My car broke down/ won't start.	**El coche se me ha averiado/no arranca.** *ehl koh·cheh seh meh ah ah·beh·reeyah·doh/ noh ah·rrahn·kah*
Can you fix it (today)?	**¿Puede arreglarlo (hoy mismo)?** *pweh·deh ah·rreh·glahr·loh (oy meez·moh)*
When will it be ready?	**¿Cuándo estará listo?** *kwahn·doh ehs·tah·rah lees·toh*
How much?	**¿Cuánto es?** *kwahn·toh ehs*
I have a puncture/ flat tyre (tire)	**Tengo un neumático pinchado/desinflado** *tehn·goh oon neoo·mah·tee·coh peen·chah·doh/ dehs·een·flah·doh*

Accidents

There was an accident.	**Ha habido un accidente.** *ah ah·bee·doh oon ahk·thee·dehn·teh*
Call an ambulance/ the police.	**Llame a una ambulancia/la policía.** *yah·meh ah oo·nah ahm·boo·lahn·theeyah/ lah poh·lee·thee·ah*

Places to Stay

ESSENTIAL

Can you recommend a hotel?	**¿Puede recomendarme un hotel?** *pweh·deh reh·koh·mehn·dahr·meh oon oh·tehl*
I have a reservation.	**Tengo una reserva.** *tehn·goh oo·nah reh·sehr·bah*
My name is…	**Me llamo…** *meh yah·moh…*
Do you have a room…?	**¿Tienen habitaciones…?** *teeyeh·nehn ah·bee·tah·theeyoh·nehs…*
for one/two	**individuales/dobles** *een·dee·bee·doo·ah·lehs/doh·blehs*
with a bathroom	**con baño** *kohn bah·nyoh*
with air conditioning	**con aire acondicionado** *kohn ayee·reh ah·kohn·dee·theeyoh·nah·doh*
For…	**Para…** *pah·rah…*
tonight	**esta noche** *ehs·tah noh·cheh*
two nights	**dos noches** *dohs noh·chehs*
one week	**una semana** *oo·nah seh·mah·nah*
How much?	**¿Cuánto es?** *kwahn·toh ehs*
Is there anything cheaper?	**¿Hay alguna tarifa más barata?** *aye ahl·goo·nah tah·ree·fah mahs bah·rah·tah*
When's check-out?	**¿A qué hora hay que desocupar la habitación?** *ah keh oh·rah aye keh deh·soh·koo·pahr lah ah·bee·tah·theeyohn*
Can I leave this in the safe?	**¿Puedo dejar esto en la caja fuerte?** *pweh·doh deh·khahr ehs·toh ehn lah kah·khah fwehr·teh*
Can I leave my bags?	**¿Podría dejar mi equipaje?** *poh·dree·ah deh·khahr mee eh·kee·pah·kheh*
Can I have the bill/ a receipt?	**¿Me da la factura/un recibo?** *meh dah lah fahk·too·rah/oon reh·thee·boh*

| I'll pay in cash/by credit card. | **Voy a pagar en efectivo/con tarjeta de crédito.** *boy ah pah·gahr ehn eh·fehk·tee·boh/ kohn tahr·kheh·tah deh kreh·dee·toh* |

If you didn't reserve accommodations before your trip, visit the local **Oficina de turismo** (Tourist Information Office) for recommendations on places to stay.

Somewhere to Stay

Can you recommend…?	**¿Puede recomendarme…** *pweh·deh reh·koh·mehn·dahr·meh*
a hotel?	**un hotel?** *oon oh·tehl*
a hostel?	**un albergue?** *oon ahl·behr·geh?*
a campsite	**un cámping?** *oon kahm·peeng?*
a bed and breakfast	**una pensión?** *oo·nah pehn·seeyohn*
What is it near?	**¿Qué hay cerca?** *keh aye thehr·kah*
How do I get there?	**¿Cómo se llega allí?** *koh·moh seh yeh·gah ah·yee*

At the Hotel

I have a reservation.	**Tengo una reserva.** _tehn_•goh _oo_•nah reh•_sehr_•bah
My name is…	**Me llamo…** meh _yah_•moh…
Do you have a room…?	**¿Tiene una habitación…?** _teeyeh_•neh _oo_•nah ah•bee•tah•_theeyohn_…
for one/two	**individual/doble** een•dee•bee•_dwahl_ /_doh_•bleh
with a toilet/shower	**con un baño/una ducha** kohn oon _bah_•nyoh/_oo_•nah _doo_•chah
with air conditioning	**con aire acondicionado** kohn _ayee_•reh ah•kohn•dee•theeyoh•_nah_•doh
with a single/double bed	**con una cama/cama de matrimonio** kohn una _kah_•mah/_kah_•mah mah•tree•_moh_•neeyoh
that's smoking/non-smoking	**para fumadores/no fumadores** _pah_•rah foo•mah•_doh_•rehs/noh foo•mah•_doh_•rehs
For…	**Para…** _pah_•rah…
tonight	**esta noche** _ehs_•tah _noh_•cheh
two nights	**dos noches** dohs _noh_•chehs
a week	**una semana** _oo_•nah seh•_mah_•nah
Does the hotel have…?	**¿Tiene el hotel…?** _teeyeh_•neh ehl oh•_tehl_…

YOU MAY HEAR…

Su pasaporte/tarjeta de crédito, por favor. soo pah•sah•_pohr_•teh/tahr•_kheh_•tah deh _kreh_•dee•toh pohr fah•_bohr_	Your passport/credit card, please.
Rellene este formulario. reh•_yeh_•neh _ehs_•teh fohr•moo•_lah_•reeyoh	Fill out this form.
Firme aquí. _feer_•meh ah•_kee_	Sign here.

There's a variety of places to stay in Spain. Hotels are rated from one to five stars, with five stars being the most expensive and having the most amenities. **Paradores** are government-run inns located throughout the country. These inns are usually castles, monasteries, palaces and other landmark buildings that have been restored and converted into hotels. Reservations are recommended far in advance for **paradores**, as they are very popular, especially in the summer months. Other unique accommodations in Spain include spas, resorts, farm house rentals, apartment rentals, villas and camping.

a computer	**un ordenador**	*oon ohr•deh•nah•<u>dohr</u>*
an elevator [a lift]	**un ascensor**	*oon ah•thehn•<u>sohr</u>*
(wireless) internet service	**acceso (inalámbrico) a Internet** *ahk•<u>theh</u>•soh (een•ah•<u>lahm</u>•bree•koh) ah een•tehr•<u>neht</u>*	
room service	**servicio de habitaciones** *sehr•<u>bee</u>•theeyoh deh ah•bee•tah•<u>theeyoh</u>•nehs*	
a pool	**una piscina**	*<u>oo</u>•nah pees•<u>thee</u>•nah*
a gym	**un gimnasio**	*oon kheem•<u>nah</u>•seeyoh*
I need...	**Necesito...**	*neh•theh•<u>see</u>•toh...*
an extra bed	**otra cama**	*<u>oh</u>•trah <u>kah</u>•mah*
a cot	**un catre**	*oon <u>kah</u>•treh*
a crib	**una cuna**	*<u>oo</u>•nah <u>koo</u>•nah*

For Numbers, see page 167.

Price

How much per night/ week?	**¿Cuánto cuesta por noche/semana?** *<u>kwahn</u>•toh <u>kwehs</u>•tah pohr <u>noh</u>•cheh/seh•<u>mah</u>•nah*
Are there any discounts?	**¿Ofrecen algún descuento?** *oh•<u>freh</u>•thehn ahl•<u>goon</u> dehs•<u>kwehn</u>•toh*

| Does that include breakfast/sales tax [VAT]? | **¿Incluye el precio el desayuno/IVA?** *een-kloo-yeh ehl preh-theeyoh ehl deh-sah-yoo-noh/eh-beh-ah* |

Preferences

Can I see the room?	**¿Puedo ver la habitación?** *pweh-doh behr lah ah-bee-tah-theeyohn*
I'd like a...room.	**Quiero una habitación...** *keeyeh-roh oo-nah ah-bee-tah-theeyohn*
better	**mejor** *meh-khohr*
bigger	**más grande** *mahs grahn-deh*
cheaper	**más barata** *mahs bah-rah-tah*
quieter	**más silenciosa** *mahs see-lehn-ceeyo-sah*
I'll take it.	**Me lo llevo** *meh loh yeh-boh*
No, I won't take it.	**No, no me lo llevo** *noh, noh meh loh yeh-boh*

Questions

Where's...?	**¿Dónde está...?** *dohn-deh ehs-tah...*
the bar	**el bar** *ehl bahr*
the bathrooms	**el baño** *ehl bah-nyoh*
the elevator [lift]	**el ascensor** *ehl ahs-thehn-sohr*
Can I have...?	**¿Puede darme...?** *pweh-deh dahr-meh...*
a blanket	**una manta** *oo-nah mahn-tah*
an iron	**una plancha** *oo-nah plahn-chah*
a pillow	**una almohada** *oo-nah ahl-moh-ah-dah*
soap	**jabón** *khah-bohn*
toilet paper	**papel higiénico** *pah-pehl ee-kheeyeh-nee-koh*
a towel	**una toalla** *oo-nah toh-ah-yah*
Do you have an adapter for this?	**¿Tiene un adaptador para esto?** *teeyeh-neh oon ah-dahp-tah-dohr pah-rah ehs-toh*
How do I turn on the lights?	**¿Cómo enciendo las luces?** *koh-moh ehn-theeyehn-doh lahs loo-thehs*

Can you wake me at…?	**¿Podría despertarme a la/las…?**
	poh·dree·ah dehs·pehr·tahr·meh ah lah/lahs…
Can I leave this in the safe?	**¿Puedo dejar esto en la caja fuerte?**
	pweh·doh deh·khahr ehs·toh ehn lah kah·khah fwehr·teh
Can I have my things from the safe?	**¿Podría darme mis cosas de la caja fuerte?**
	poh·dree·ah dahr·meh mees koh·sahs deh lah kah·khah fwehr·teh
Is there mail [post]/ a message for me?	**¿Hay correo/algún mensaje para mí?**
	aye koh·rreh·oh/ahl·goon mehn·sah·kheh pah·rah mee

> When asking for a public restroom, it's more common and polite to use the term **servicio**. The term **baño** tends to be used when asking for a private bathroom such as in a home or a hotel room. Native speakers sometimes use both words interchangeably, but you will almost always see **servicio** on a sign.

YOU MAY SEE…

EMPUJAR/TIRAR	push/pull
BAÑO/SERVICIO	bathroom/restroom [toilet]
DUCHA	shower
ASCENSOR	elevator [lift]
ESCALERAS	stairs
LAVANDERÍA	laundry
NO MOLESTAR	do not disturb
PUERTA DE INCENDIOS	fire door
SALIDA (DE EMERGENCIA)	(emergency) exit
LLAMADA DESPERTADOR	wake-up call

| Do you have a laundry service? | **¿Tienen servicio de lavandería?** |
| | *teeyeh•nehn sehr•bee•theeyoh deh lah•bahn•deh•ree•ah* |

For Grammar, see page 162.

Problems

There's a problem.	**Hay un problema.** *aye oon proh•bleh•mah*
I lost my key/ key card.	**He perdido la llave/llave electrónica.** *eh pehr•dee•doh lah yah•beh/yah•beh eh•lehk•troh•nee•kah*
I've locked my key/ key card in the room.	**He dejado la llave dentro de la habitación.** *eh deh•khah•doh lah yah•beh dehn•troh deh lah ah•bee•tah•theeyohn*
There's no hot water/toilet paper.	**No hay agua caliente/papel higiénico.** *no aye ah•gwah kah•leeyehn•teh/pah•pehl ee•kheeyeh•nee•koh*
The room is dirty.	**La habitación está sucia.** *lah ah•bee•tah•theeyohn ehs•tah soo•theeyah*
There are bugs in the room.	**Hay insectos en la habitación.** *aye een•sehk•tohs ehn lah ah•bee•tah•theeyohn*
...doesn't work.	**...no funciona.** *... no foon•theeyoh•nah*
Can you fix...?	**¿Pueden arreglar...?** *pweh•dehn ah•rreh•glahr...*
the air conditioning	**el aire acondicionado** *ehl ayee•reh ah•kohn•dee•theeyoh•nah•doh*
the fan	**el ventilador** *ehl behn•tee•lah•dohr*
the heat [heating]	**la calefacción** *lah kah•leh•fahk•theeyohn*
the light	**la luz** *lah looth*
the TV	**la televisión** *lah teh•leh•bee•seeyohn*
the toilet	**el retrete** *ehl reh•treh•teh*
I'd like another room.	**Quiero otra habitación.** *keeyeh•roh oh•trah ah•bee•tah•theeyohn*

43

Spain's electricity is 220 volts. You may need a converter and/or an adapter for your appliances.

Checking Out

When's check-out?	**¿A qué hora hay que desocupar la habitación?** *ah keh oh•rah aye keh deh•soh•koo•pahr lah ah•bee•tah•theeyohn*
Can I leave my bags here until…?	**¿Puedo dejar mi equipaje aquí hasta…?** *pweh•doh deh•khahr mee eh•kee•pah•kheh ah•kee ahs•tah…*
Can I have an itemized bill/a receipt?	**¿Puede darme una factura detallada/un recibo?** *pweh•deh dahr•meh oo•nah fahk•too•rah deh•tah•yah•dah/oon reh•thee•boh*
I think there's a mistake.	**Creo que hay un error.** *kreh•oh keh aye oon eh•rrohr*
I made… phone calls.	**He hecho…llamadas.** *eh eh•choh… yah•mah•dahs*
I took…from the mini-bar.	**He tomado…del minibar.** *eh toh•mah•doh… dehl mee•nee•bar*
I'll pay in cash/ by credit card.	**Voy a pagar en efectivo/con tarjeta de crédito.** *boy ah pah•gahr ehn eh•fehk•tee•boh/ kohn tahr•kheh•tah deh kreh•dee•toh*

Tipping in hotels, restaurants and bars isn't customary in Spain. However, if you wish to leave a tip for good service, it will be appreciated; just round up a bill to the nearest euro or two.

Renting

I reserved an apartment/a room.	**He reservado un apartamento/una habitación.** *eh reh·sehr·bah·doh oon ah·pahr·tah·mehn·toh/ oo·nah ah·bee·tah·theeyohn*
My name is…	**Me llamo…** *meh yah·moh…*
Can I have the key/key card?	**¿Puede darme la llave/llave electrónica?** *pweh·deh dahr·meh lah yah·beh/ yah·beh eh·lehk·troh·nee·kah*
Are there…?	**¿Hay…?** *aye…*
dishes	**platos** *plah·tohs*
pillows	**almohadas** *ahl·moh·ah·dahs*
sheets	**sábanas** *sah·bah·nahs*
towels	**toallas** *toh·ah·yahs*
kitchen utensils	**cubiertos** *koo·beeyehr·tohs*
When do I put out the bins/recycling?	**¿Cuándo saco la basura/el reciclado?** *kwahn·doh sah·koh lah bah·soo·rah/ ehl reh·thee·klah·doh*
…is broken.	**…está estropeado *m*/estropeada *f*.** *…ehs·tah ehs·troh·peh·ah·doh/ehs·troh·peh·ah·dah*
How does… work?	**¿Cómo funciona…?** *koh·moh foon·theeyoh*
the air conditioner	**el aire acondicionado** *ehl ayee·reh ah·kohn·dee·theeyoh·nah·doh*
the dishwasher	**el lavavajillas** *ehl lah·bah·bah·khee·yahs*
the freezer	**el congelador** *ehl kohn·kheh·lah·dohr*
the heater	**la calefacción** *lah kah·leh·fahk·theeyohn*
the microwave	**el microondas** *ehl mee·kroh·ohn·dahs*
the refrigerator	**la nevera** *lah neh·beh·rah*
the stove	**el horno** *ehl ohr·noh*
the washing machine	**la lavadora** *lah lah·bah·doh·rah*

Domestic Items

I need...	**Necesito...** neh·theh·<u>see</u>·toh...
an adapter	**un adaptador** oon ah·dahp·tah·<u>dohr</u>
aluminum	**papel de aluminio** pah·<u>pehl</u> deh
[kitchen] foil	ah·loo·<u>mee</u>·neeyoh
a bottle opener	**un abrebotellas** oon ah·breh·boh·teh·<u>teh</u>·yahs
a broom	**una escoba** <u>oo</u>·nah ehs·<u>koh</u>·bah
a can opener	**un abrelatas** oon ah·breh·<u>lah</u>·tahs
cleaning supplies	**productos de limpieza**
	proh·<u>dook</u>·tohs deh leem·<u>peeyeh</u>·thah
a corkscrew	**un sacacorchos** oon sah·kah·<u>kohr</u>·chohs
detergent	**detergente** deh·tehr·<u>khehn</u>·teh
dishwashing	**líquido lavavajillas** lee·kee·doh
liquid	lah·bah·bah·<u>khee</u>·yahs
bin bags	**bolsas de basura** <u>bohl</u>·sahs deh bah·<u>soo</u>·rah
a lightbulb	**una bombilla** <u>oo</u>·nah bohm·<u>bee</u>·yah
matches	**cerillas** theh·<u>ree</u>·yahs
a mop	**una fregona** <u>oo</u>·nah freh·<u>goh</u>·nah
napkins	**servilletas** sehr·bee·<u>yeh</u>·tahs
paper towels	**papel de cocina** pah·<u>pehl</u> deh koh·<u>thee</u>·nah
plastic wrap	**film transparente** feelm
[cling film]	trahns·pah·<u>rehn</u>·teh
a plunger	**un desatascador** oon deh·sah·tahs·kah·<u>dohr</u>
scissors	**tijeras** tee·<u>kheh</u>·rahs
a vacuum cleaner	**una aspiradora** <u>oo</u>·nah ahs·pee·rah·<u>doh</u>·rah

For In the Kitchen, see page 80.

At the Hostel

| Is there a bed available? | **¿Hay camas disponibles?** aye <u>kah</u>·mahs dees·poh·<u>nee</u>·blehs |
| I'd like... | **¿Me puede dar...?** meh <u>pweh</u>·deh dahr... |

With more than 100 hostels around Spain, finding an inexpensive place to stay should be easy. Hostels are inexpensive accommodations that have dormitory-style rooms and, sometimes, private or semi-private rooms. Some offer private bathrooms, though most have shared facilities. There is usually a self-service kitchen on site. Reservations are recommended in advance in larger cities and popular destinations during the tourist season.

a single/ double room	**una habitación individual/doble** _oo_•nah ah•bee•tah•_theeyohn_ een•dee•bee•doo•_ahl_/_doh_•bleh
a blanket	**una manta** _oo_•nah _mahn_•tah
a pillow	**una almohada** _oo_•nah ahl•moh•_ah_•dah
sheets	**sábanas** _sah_•bah•nahs
a towel	**una toalla** _oo_•nah toh•_ah_•yah
Do you have lockers?	**¿Tienen consignas?** _teeyeh_•nehn kohn•_seeg_•nahs
When do you lock up?	**¿A qué hora cierran las puertas?** ah keh _oh_•rah _theeyeh_•rrahn lahs _pwehr_•tahs
Do I need a membership card?	**¿Necesito una tarjeta de socio?** neh•theh•_see_•toh _oo_•nah tahr•_kheh_•tah de _soh_•theeyoh
Here's my International Student Card.	**Aquí tiene mi carnet internacional de estudiante.** ah•_kee teeyeh_•neh mee kahr•_neht_ een•tehr•nah•theeyoh•_nahl_ deh ehs•too•_deeyahn_•teh

Going Camping

Can I camp here?	**¿Puedo acampar aquí?** _pweh_•doh ah•kahm•_pahr_ ah•_kee_
Where's the campsite?	**¿Dónde está el cámping?** _dohn_•deh ehs•_tah_ ehl _kahm_•peeng

What is the charge per day/week?	**¿Cuánto cobran por día/semana?** _kwahn_•toh _koh_•brahn pohr _dee_•ah/seh•_mah_•nah
Are there…?	**¿Hay…?** _aye_…
cooking facilities	**instalaciones para cocinar** eens•tah•lah•_theeyoh_•nehs pah•rah koh•thee•_nahr_
electric outlets	**enchufes eléctricos** ehn•_choo_•fehs eh•_lehk_•tree•kohs
laundry facilities	**servicio de lavandería** sehr•_bee_•theeyoh deh lah•bahn•deh•_ree_•ah
showers	**duchas** _doo_•chahs
tents for hire	**tiendas de alquiler** _teeyehn_•dahs deh ahl•kee•_lehr_
Where can I empty the chemical toilet?	**¿Dónde puedo vaciar el váter químico?** _dohn_•deh _pweh_•doh bah•thee•_ahr_ ehl _bah_•tehr _kee_•mee•koh

For Domestic Items, see page 46.

YOU MAY SEE…

AGUA POTABLE	drinking water
PROHIBIDO ACAMPAR	no camping
PROHIBIDO HACER HOGUERAS/BARBACOAS	no fires/barbecues

ESSENTIAL

Where's an internet cafe?	**¿Dónde hay un cibercafé?** <u>dohn</u>·deh aye oon thee·behr·kah·<u>feh</u>
Can I access the internet/check e-mail?	**¿Puedo acceder a Internet/revisar el correo electrónico?** <u>pweh</u>·doh ahk·theh·<u>dehr</u> ah een·tehr·<u>neht</u>/reh·bee·<u>sahr</u> ehl koh·<u>rreh</u>·oh eh·lehk·<u>troh</u>·nee·koh
How much per (half) hour?	**¿Cuánto cuesta por (media) hora?** <u>kwahn</u>·toh <u>kwehs</u>·tah pohr (<u>meh</u>·deeyah) <u>oh</u>·rah
How do I connect/ log on?	**¿Cómo entro al sistema/inicio la sesión?** <u>koh</u>·moh <u>ehn</u>·troh ahl sees·<u>teh</u>·mah/ ee·nee·<u>theeyoh</u> lah seh·<u>seeyohn</u>
A phone card, please.	**Una tarjeta telefónica, por favor.** <u>oo</u>·nah tahr·<u>kheh</u>·tah teh·leh·<u>foh</u>·nee·kah pohr fah·<u>bohr</u>
Can I have your phone number?	**¿Me puede dar su número de teléfono?** meh <u>pweh</u>·deh dahr soo <u>noo</u>·meh·roh deh teh·<u>leh</u>·foh·noh
Here's my number/ e-mail address.	**Aquí tiene mi número/dirección de correo electrónico.** ah·<u>kee</u> <u>teeyeh</u>·neh mee <u>noo</u>·meh·roh/ dee·rehk·<u>theeyohn</u> deh koh·<u>rreh</u>·oh eh·lehk·<u>troh</u>·nee·koh
Call me.	**Llámeme.** <u>yah</u>·meh·meh
E-mail me.	**Envíeme un correo.** ehn·<u>bee</u>·eh·meh oon koh·<u>rreh</u>·oh
Hello. This is...	**Hola. Soy...** <u>oh</u>·lah soy...
Can I speak to...?	**¿Puedo hablar con...?** <u>pweh</u>·doh ah·<u>blahr</u> kohn...
Can you repeat that?	**¿Puede repetir eso?** <u>pweh</u>·deh reh·peh·<u>teer</u> <u>eh</u>·soh

I'll call back later.	**Llamaré más tarde.** yah·mah·_reh_ mahs _tahr_·deh
Bye.	**Adiós.** ah·_deeyohs_
Where's the post office?	**¿Dónde está la oficina de correos?** _dohn_·deh ehs·_tah_ lah oh·fee·_thee_·nah deh koh·_rreh_·ohs
I'd like to send this to…	**Quiero mandar esto a…** _keeyeh_·roh mahn·_dahr_ ehs·toh ah…

Online

Where's an internet cafe?	**¿Dónde hay un cibercafé?** _dohn_·deh aye oon thee·behr·kah·_feh_
Does it have wireless internet?	**¿Tiene Internet inalámbrico?** _teeyeh_·neh een·tehr·_neht_ een·ah·_lahm_·bree·koh
What is the WiFi password?	**¿Cuál es la contraseña de WiFI?** kwahl ehs lah kohn·trah·seh·nyah deh weeh·feeh
Is the WiFi free?	**¿Es gratuito el acceso WiFi?** esh grah·_too_·ee·toh ehl ahk·_theh_·soh weeh·feeh
Do you have bluetooth?	**¿Tiene Bluetooth?** _teeyeh_·neh blue·tooth
How do I turn the computer on/off?	**¿Cómo enciendo/apago el ordenador?** _koh_·moh ehn·_theeyen_·doh/ah·_pah_·goh ehl ohr·deh·nah·_dohr_
Can I…?	**¿Puedo…?** _pweh_·doh…
access the internet	**acceder a Internet** ahk·theh·_dehr_ ah een·tehr·_neht_
check e-mail	**revisar el correo electrónico** reh·bee·_sahr_ ehl koh·_rreh_·oh eh·lehk·_troh_·nee·koh
print	**imprimir** eem·pree·_meer_
plug in/charge my laptop/iPhone/iPad/BlackBerry?	**enchufar/cargar el portátil/iPhone/iPad/Blackberry?** ehn·choo·fahr/kahr·gahr ehl pohr·tah·teel/i·fon/i·pad/Blackberry

access Skype?	**acceder a Skype?** *ahk·theh·dehr ah skype*
How much per (half) hour?	**¿Cuánto cuesta por (media) hora?**
	kwahn·toh kwehs·tah pohr (meh·deeyah) oh·rah
How do I…?	**¿Cómo…?** *koh·moh…*
connect/ disconnect	**me conecto/me desconecto**
	meh koh·nehk·toh/meh dehs·koh·nehk·toh
log on/off	**inicio/cierro la sesión** *ee·nee·theeyoh/*
	theeyeh·rroh lah seh·seeyohn
type this symbol	**escribo este símbolo** *ehs·kree·boh ehs·teh seem·boh·loh*
What's your e-mail?	**¿Cuál es su dirección de correo electrónico?**
	kwahl ehs soo dee·rehk·theeyohn deh
	koh·rreh·oh eh·lehk·troh·nee·koh
My e-mail is…	**Mi dirección de correo electrónico es…**
	mee dee·rehk·theeyohn deh koh·rreh·oh
	eh·lehk·troh·nee·koh ehs…

Do you have a scanner? **¿Tienen un escáner?** *teeyeh·nehn oon ehs·kah·nehr*

Social Media

Are you on Facebook/ Twitter?	**¿Está en Facebook/Twitter?** *(polite form)*
	ehs·tah ehn Facebook/Twitter
	¿Estás en Facebook/Twitter? *(informal form)*
	ehs·tahs ehn Facebook/Twitter
What's your user name?	**¿Cuál es su nombre de usuario?** *(polite form)*
	kwahl ehs soo nohm·breh deh oo·soo·ah·reeyoh
	¿Cuál es tu nombre de usuario? *(informal form)*
	kwahl ehs too nohm·breh deh
	oo·soo·ah·reeyoh
I'll add you as a friend.	**Le añadiré como amigo.** *(polite form)*
	leh ah·nyah·dee·reh koh·moh ah·mee·goh
	Te añadiré como amigo. *(informal form)*
	teh ah·nyah·dee·reh koh·moh ah·mee·goh

YOU MAY SEE…

CERRAR	close
BORRAR	delete
CORREO ELECTRÓNICO	e-mail
SALIR	exit
AYUDA	help
MENSAJERO INSTANTÁNEO	instant messenger
INTERNET	internet
INICIO DE SESIÓN	login
NUEVO (MENSAJE)	new (message)
ENCENDER/APAGAR	on/off
ABRIR	open
IMPRIMIR	print
GUARDAR	save
ENVIAR	send
NOMBRE DE USUARIO/CONTRASEÑA	username/password
INTERNET INALÁMBRICO	wireless internet

I'll follow you on Twitter. **Le seguiré en Twitter.** *(polite form)*
leh seh·gee·reh ehn Twitter

Te seguiré en Twitter. *(informal form)*
teh seh·gee·reh ehn Twitter

Are you following…? **¿Sigue a…?** *(polite form)* *see·geh ah*

¿Sigues a…? *(informal form)* *see·gehs ah*

I'll put the pictures on Facebook/Twitter. **Subiré las fotos a Facebook/Twitter.**
soo·bee·reh lahs foh·tohs ah Facebook/Twitter

I'll tag you in the pictures. **Le etiquetaré en las fotos.** *(polite form)*
leh eh·tee·keh·tah·reh ehn lahs foh·tohs

Te etiquetaré en las fotos. *(informal form)*
teh eh·tee·keh·tah·reh ehn lahs foh·tohs

Phone

A phone card/ prepaid phone, please.	**Una tarjeta telefónica/Un teléfono prepago, por favor.** *oo•nah tahr•<u>kheh</u>•tah teh•leh•<u>foh</u>•nee•kah/ oon teh•<u>leh</u>•foh•noh preh•<u>pah</u>•goh pohr fah•<u>bohr</u>*
How much?	**¿Cuánto es?** *<u>kwahn</u>•toh ehs*
Where's the pay phone?	**¿Dónde está el teléfono público?** *dohn•deh ehs•tah ehl teh•leh•foh•noh poo•blee•koh*
What's the area code/ country code for…?	**¿Cuál es el prefijo/código de país para…?** *kwahl ehs ehl preh•<u>fee</u>•khoh/<u>koh</u>•dee•goh deh pah•<u>ees</u> pah•rah…*
What's the number for Information?	**¿Cuál es el número de información?** *kwahl ehs ehl <u>noo</u>•meh•roh deh een•fohr•mah•<u>theeyohn</u>*
I'd like the number for…	**Quiero que me dé el número de teléfono de…** *keeyeh•roh keh meh deh ehl <u>noo</u>•meh•roh deh teh•<u>leh</u>•foh•noh deh…*
I'd like to call collect [reverse the charges].	**Quiero llamar a cobro revertido** *keeyeh•roh yah•mahr ah koh•broh reh•behr•tee•doh*
My phone doesn't work here.	**Mi teléfono no funciona aquí.** *mee teh•<u>leh</u>•foh•noh no foon•<u>theeyoh</u>•nah ah•<u>kee</u>*
What network are you on?	**¿En qué red está?** *ehn keh rehd ehs•tah*
Is it 3G?	**¿Es 3G?** *ehs trehs kheh*
I have run out of credit/minutes.	**Me he quedado sin saldo/minutos.** *meh eh keh•dah•doh seen sahl•doh/meeh•noo•tohs*
Can I buy some credit?	**¿Puedo comprar una recarga de saldo?** *pweh•doh kohm•prahr oo•nah reh•kahr•gah deh sahl•doh*
Do you have a phone charger?	**¿Tiene un cargador de móvil?** *teeyeh•neh oon kahr•gah•dohr deh moh•beel*
Can I have your number?	**¿Me puede dar su número de teléfono?** *meh <u>pweh</u>•deh dahr soo <u>noo</u>•meh•roh deh teh•<u>leh</u>•foh•noh*
Here's my number.	**Aquí tiene mi número.** *ah•<u>kee</u> teeyeh•neh mee <u>noo</u>•meh•roh*

Please call me.	**Llámame, por favor.** _yah·mah·meh pohr fah·bohr_
Please text me.	**Envíame un mensaje de texto, por favor.**
	ehn·beeyah·meh oon mehn·sah·kheh deh tehx·toh pohr fah·bohr
I'll call you.	**Le _m_ /La _f_ llamaré.** _leh/lah yah·mah·reh_
I'll text you.	**Te enviaré un mensaje de texto.**
	teh ehn·beeyah·reh oon mehn·sah·kheh deh tehx·toh

Telephone Etiquette

Hello. This is…	**Hola. Soy…** _oh·lah soy…_
Can I speak to…?	**¿Puedo hablar con…?** _pweh·doh ah·blahr kohn…_
Extension…	**Extensión…** _ehks·tehn·seeyohn…_
Speak louder/more slowly, please.	**Hable más alto/despacio, por favor.** _ah·bleh mahs ahl·toh/dehs·pah·theeyoh pohr fah·bohr_

Public phones are either coin- or card-operated, though coin-operated phones are becoming less common. Phone cards can be purchased in post offices, newsstands and tobacconists. For international calls, calling cards are the most economical. You can also make your long-distance calls at **locutorios** (call centers); these additionally offer internet, fax and wireless phone-charging services at reasonable prices. Calling internationally from your hotel may be convenient, but the rates can be very expensive.

Important telephone numbers:

emergencies, 112

information, 010

operator assistance, 025

To call the U.S. or Canada from Spain, dial 00 + 1 + area code + phone number. To call the U.K. from Spain, dial 00 + 44 + area code (minus the first 0) + phone number.

YOU MAY HEAR...

¿Quién llama? *keeyehn yah·mah* — Who's calling?

Espere. *ehs·peh·reh* — Hold on.

Le paso. *leh pah·soh* — I'll put you through.

No está. *noh ehs·tah* — He/She is not here.

No puede atenderle en este momento. *noh pweh·deh ah·tehn·dehr·leh ehn ehs·teh moh·mehn·toh* — He/She can't come to the phone.

¿Quiere dejarle un mensaje? *keeyeh·reh deh·khahr·leh oon mehn·sah·kheh* — Would you like to leave a message?

Vuelva a llamar más tarde/en diez minutos. *bwehl·bah ah yah·mahr mahs tahr·deh/ehn deeyeth mee·noo·tohs* — Call back later/in 10 minutes.

¿Le puede llamar él m/ella f a usted? *leh pweh·deh yah·mahr ehl/eh·yah ah oos·tehth* — Can he/she call you back?

¿Me da su número? *meh dah soo noo·meh·roh* — What's your number?

Can you repeat that?	**¿Puede repetir eso?** *pweh·deh reh·peh·teer eh·soh*
I'll call back later.	**Llamaré más tarde.** *yah·mah·reh mahs tahr·deh*
Bye.	**Adiós.** *ah·deeyohs*

For Business Travel, see page 142.

Fax

Can I send/receive a fax here?	**¿Puedo enviar/recibir un fax aquí?** *pweh·doh ehn·bee·ahr/reh·thee·beer oon fahx ah·kee*
What's the fax number?	**¿Cuál es el número de fax?** *kwahl ehs ehl noo·meh·roh deh fahx*
Please fax this to…	**Por favor envíe este fax a…** *pohr fah·bohr ehn·bee·eh ehs·teh fahx ah…*

Post

Where's the post office/mailbox?	**¿Dónde está la oficina/el buzón de correos?** _dohn_•deh ehs•_tah_ lah oh•fee•_thee_•nah/ ehl boo•_thohn_ deh koh•_rreh_•ohs
A stamp for this postcard/letter to...	**Un sello para esta postal/carta a...** oon _seh_•yoh _pah_•rah ehs•tah pohs•_tahl_/_kahr_•tah ah...
How much?	**¿Cuánto es?** _kwahn_•toh ehs
I want to send this package by airmail/express.	**Quiero mandar este paquete por correo aéreo/urgente.** _keeyeh_•roh mahn•_dahr_ ehs•teh pah•_keh_•teh pohr koh•_rreh_•oh ah•_eh_•reh•oh/oor•_khen_•teh
A receipt, please.	**Un recibo, por favor.** oon reh•_thee_•boh pohr fah•_bohr_

YOU MAY HEAR...

Rellene la declaración para la aduana. reh•_yeh_•neh lah deh•klah•rah•_theeyohn_ _pah_•rah lah ah•doo•_ah_•nah	Fill out the customs declaration form.
¿Qué valor tiene? keh bah•_lohr_ _teeyeh_•neh	What's the value?
¿Qué hay dentro? keh aye _dehn_•troh	What's inside?

Oficinas de Correos (post offices) in Spain offer more than just standard postal services. You may be able to fax, scan and e-mail documents and send money orders from the local post office. Services available vary by location.

Food & Drink

Eating Out

ESSENTIAL

Can you recommend a good restaurant/bar?	**¿Puede recomendarme un buen restaurante/bar?** _pweh·deh reh·koh·mehn·dahr·meh oon bwehn rehs·taw·rahn·teh/bahr_
Is there a traditional Spanish/an inexpensive restaurant nearby?	**¿Hay un restaurante típico español/barato cerca de aquí?** _aye oon rehs·taw·rahn·teh tee·pee·koh ehs·pah·nyohl/bah·rah·toh thehr·kah deh ah·kee_
A table for..., please.	**Una mesa para..., por favor.** _oo·nah meh·sah pah·rah...pohr fah·bohr_
Can we sit...?	**¿Podemos sentarnos...?** _poh·deh·mohs sehn·tahr·nohs..._
here/there	**aquí/allí** _ah·kee/ah·yee_
outside	**fuera** _fweh·rah_
in a non-smoking area	**en una zona de no fumadores** _ehn oo·nah thoh·nah deh noh foo·mah·doh·rehs_
I'm waiting for someone.	**Estoy esperando a alguien.** _ehs·toy ehs·peh·rahn·doh ah ahl·geeyehn_
Where are the toilets?	**¿Dónde están los servicios?** _dohn·deh ehs·tahn lohs sehr·bee·theeyohs_
A menu, please.	**Una carta, por favor.** _oo·nah kahr·tah pohr fah·bohr_
What do you recommend?	**¿Qué me recomienda?** _keh meh reh·koh·meeyehn·dah_
I'd like...	**Quiero...** _keeyeh·roh..._
Some more..., please.	**Quiero más..., por favor.** _keeyeh·roh mahs...pohr fah·bohr_

Enjoy your meal!	**¡Que aproveche!** *keh ah·proh·beh·cheh*
The check [bill], please.	**La cuenta, por favor.** *lah kwen·tah pohr fah·bohr*
Is service included?	**¿Está incluido el servicio?** *ehs·tah een·kloo·ee·doh ehl sehr·bee·theeyoh*
Can I pay by credit card?	**¿Puedo pagar con tarjeta de crédito?** *pweh·doh pah·gahr kohn tahr·kheh·tah deh kreh·dee·toh*
Can I have a receipt?	**¿Podría darme un recibo?** *poh·dree·ah dahr·meh oon reh·thee·boh*
Thank you!	**¡Gracias!** *grah·theeyahs*

Where to Eat

Can you recommend...?	**¿Puede recomendarme...?** *pweh·deh reh·koh·mehn·dahr·meh...*
a restaurant	**un restaurante** *oon rehs·taw·rahn·teh*
a bar	**un bar** *oon bahr*
a cafe	**un café** *oon kah·feh*
a fast-food place	**un restaurante de comida rápida** *oon rehs·taw·rahn·teh deh koh·mee·dah rah·pee·dah*
a tapas bar	**un bar de tapas** *oon bahr deh tah·pahs*
a cheap restaurant	**un restaurante barato** *oon rehs·taw·rahn·teh bah·rah·toh*
an expensive restaurant	**un restaurante caro** *oon rehs·taw·rahn·teh kah·roh*
a restaurant with a good view	**un restaurante con buenas vistas** *oon rehs·taw·rahn·teh kohn bweh·nash bees·tahs*
an authentic/ a non-touristy restaurant	**un restaurante auténtico/no turístico** *oon rehs·taw·rahn·teh awtehn·tee·koh/ noh too·reesh·tee·koh*

Reservations & Preferences

I'd like to reserve a table...	**Quiero reservar una mesa...** _keeyeh_•roh _reh_•sehr•_bahr_ _oo_•nah _meh_•sah...
for two	**para dos** _pah_•rah dohs
for this evening	**para esta noche** _pah_•rah _ehs_•tah _noh_•cheh
for tomorrow at...	**para mañana a la/las...** _pah_•rah mah•_nyah_•nah ah lah/lahs...
A table for two, please.	**Una mesa para dos, por favor.** _oo_•nah _meh_•sah _pah_•rah dohs pohr fah•_bohr_
We have a reservation.	**Tenemos una reserva.** teh•_neh_•mohs _oo_•nah reh•_sehr_•bah
My name is...	**Me llamo...** meh _yah_•moh...
Can we sit...?	**¿Podríamos sentarnos...?** poh•_dree_•ah•mohs sehn•_tahr_•nohs...
here/there	**aquí/allí** ah•_kee_/ah•_yee_
outside	**fuera** _fweh_•rah
in a non-smoking area	**en una zona de no fumadores** ehn _oo_•nah _thoh_•nah deh noh foo•mah•_doh_•rehs
by the window	**al lado de la ventana** ahl _lah_•doh de lah behn•_tah_•nah

YOU MAY HEAR...

¿Tiene reserva?	Do you have
teeyeh•neh reh•sehr•bah	a reservation?
¿Cuántos son? _kwahn•tohs sohn_	How many?
¿Fumador o no fumador?	Smoking or
foo•mah•dohr oh noh foo•mah•dohr	non-smoking?
¿Está listo _m_ /lista _f_ para pedir?	Are you ready to order?
ehs•tah lees•toh/lees•tah pah•rah peh•deer	
¿Qué va a tomar? _keh bah ah toh•mahr_	What would you like?
Le recomiendo... _leh reh•koh•meeyehn•doh..._	I recommend...
Que aproveche. _keh ah•proh•beh•cheh_	Enjoy your meal.

in the shade/sun	**¿Me puede dar una mesa a la sombra/al sol?**
	meh pweh•deh dahr oo•nah meh•sah
	ah lah sohm•brah/ahl sohl
Where are the toilets?	**¿Dónde están los servicios?** _dohn•deh ehs•tahn_
	lohs sehr•bee•theeyohs

For Grammar, see page 162.

How to Order

Waiter/Waitress!	**¡Camarero _m_ /Camarera _f_ !** _kah•mah•reh•roh/_
	kah•mah•reh•rah
We're ready to order.	**Estamos listos para pedir.** _ehs•tah•mohs_
	lees•tohs pah•rah peh•deer
May I see the	**La carta de vinos, por favor.** _lah kahr•tah deh_
wine list?	_bee•nohs pohr fah•bohr_
I'd like...	**Quiero...** _keeyeh•roh..._
a bottle of...	**una botella de...** _oo•nah boh•teh•yah deh..._
a carafe of...	**una garrafa de...** _oo•nah gah•rrah•fah deh..._

a glass of…	**un vaso de…**	*oon bah•soh deh…*
Can I have a menu?	**La carta, por favor.**	*lah kahr•tah pohr fah•bohr*
Do you have…?	**¿Tiene…?**	*teeyeh•neh…*
a menu in English	**una carta en inglés**	*oo•nah kahr•tah ehn een•glehs*
a fixed-price menu	**el menú del día**	*ehl meh•noo dehl dee•ah*
a children's menu	**una carta para niños**	*oo•nah kahr•tah pah•rah nee•nyohs*
What do you recommend?	**¿Qué me recomienda?**	*keh meh reh•koh•meeyehn•dah*
What's this?	**¿Qué es esto?**	*keh ehs ehs•toh*
What's in it?	**¿Qué lleva?**	*keh yeh•bah*
Is it spicy?	**¿Es picante?**	*ehs pee•kahn•teh*
I'd like…	**Quiero…**	*keeyeh•roh…*
More…, please.	**Más…, por favor.**	*mahs…pohr fah•bohr*
With/Without…	**Con/Sin…**	*kohn/seen…*
I can't have…	**No puedo tomar…**	*noh pweh•doh toh•mahr…*
rare	**muy poco hecho *m*/hecha *f***	*mooy poh•koh eh•choh/eh•chah*
medium	**medio hecho *m*/hecha *f***	*meh•deeyoh eh•choh/eh•chah*
well-done	**bien hecho *m*/hecha *f***	*beeyehn eh•choh/eh•chah*
It's to go [take away].	**Es para llevar.**	*ehs pah•rah yeh•bahr*

For Drinks, see page 82.

YOU MAY SEE…

CARTA	menu
MENÚ DEL DÍA	menu of the day
SERVICIO (NO) INCLUIDO	service (not) included
ESPECIALIDADES DE LA CASA	specials

Cooking Methods

baked	**al horno**	ahl <u>ohr</u>•noh
boiled	**hervido** m/**hervida** f	ehr•<u>bee</u>•doh/ehr•<u>bee</u>•da
braised	**a fuego lento**	ah <u>fweh</u>•goh <u>lehn</u>•toh
breaded	**empanado** m/**empanada** f	ehm•pah•<u>nah</u>•doh/ ehm•pah•<u>nah</u>•dah
creamed	**con nata**	kohn <u>nah</u>•tah
diced	**cortado en taquitos**	kohr•<u>tah</u>•doh ehn tah•<u>kee</u>•tohs
fileted	**cortado en filetes**	kohr•<u>tah</u>•doh ehn fee•<u>leh</u>•tehs
fried	**frito** m/**frita** f	<u>free</u>•toh/<u>free</u>•tah
grilled	**a la plancha**	ah lah <u>plahn</u>•chah
poached	**escalfado** m/**escalfada** f	ehs•kahl•<u>fah</u>•doh/ ehs•kahl•<u>fah</u>•dah
roasted	**asado** m/**asada** f	ah•<u>sah</u>•doh/ah•<u>sah</u>•dah
sautéed	**salteado** m/**salteada** f	sahl•teh•<u>ah</u>•doh/sahl•teh•<u>ah</u>•dah
smoked	**ahumado** m/**ahumada** f	ah•oo•<u>mah</u>•doh/ ah•oo•<u>mah</u>•dah
steamed	**al vapor**	ahl bah•<u>pohr</u>
stewed	**guisado** m/**guisada** f	gee•<u>sah</u>•doh/gee•<u>sah</u>•dah
stuffed	**relleno** m/**rellena** f	reh•<u>yeh</u>•noh/reh•<u>yeh</u>•nah

Dietary Requirements

I'm…	**Soy…**	soy…
diabetic	**diabético** m/**diabética** f	dee•ah•<u>beh</u>•tee•koh/ dee•ah•<u>beh</u>•tee•kah
lactose intolerant	**alérgico** m/**alérgica** f **a la lactosa**	ah•<u>lehr</u>•khee•koh/ah•<u>lehr</u>•khee•kah ah lah lahk•<u>toh</u>•sah
vegetarian	**vegetariano** m/**vegetariana** f	beh•kheh•tah•<u>reeyah</u>•noh/beh•kheh•tah•<u>reeyah</u>•nah
I'm allergic to…	**Soy alérgico** m/**alérgica** f **a…**	soy ah•<u>lehr</u>•khee•koh/ah•<u>lehr</u>•khee•kah ah…

I can't eat...	**No puedo comer...** _noh pweh-doh koh-mehr..._
dairy products	**productos lácteos** _proh-dook-tohs lahk-teh-ohs_
gluten	**gluten** _gloo-tehn_
nuts	**frutos secos** _froo-tohs seh-kohs_
pork	**carne de cerdo** _kahr-neh deh thehr-doh_
shellfish	**marisco** _mah-rees-koh_
spicy foods	**comidas picantes** _koh-mee-dahs pee-kahn-tehs_
wheat	**trigo** _tree-goh_
Is it halal/kosher?	**¿Es halal/kosher?** _ehs ah-lahl/koh-sehr_
Do you have...?	**¿Tiene...?** _teeyeh-neh_
skimmed milk	**leche desnatada** _leh-cheh dehs-nah-tah-dah_
whole milk	**leche entera** _leh-cheh ehn-teh-rah_
soya milk	**leche de soja** _leh-cheh deh soh-khah_

Dining with Children

Do you have children's portions?	**¿Sirven raciones para niños?** _seer-behn rah-theeyoh-nehs pah-rah nee-nyohs_
Can I have a highchair/child's seat?	**Una trona/silla para niños, por favor.** _oo-nah troh-nah/see-yah pah-rah nee-nyohs pohr fah-bohr_
Where can I feed/change the baby?	**¿Dónde puedo darle de comer/cambiar al niño?** _dohn-deh pweh-doh dahr-leh deh koh-mehr/kahm-beeyahr ahl nee-nyoh_
Can you warm this?	**¿Puede calentar esto?** _pweh-deh kah-lehn-tahr ehs-toh_

For Traveling with Children, see page 144.

How to Complain

When will our food be ready?	**¿Cuánto más tardará la comida?** _kwahn-toh mahs tahr-dah-rah lah koh-mee-dah_
We can't wait any longer.	**No podemos esperar más.** _noh poh-deh-mohs ehs-peh-rahr mahs_
We're leaving.	**Nos vamos.** _nohs bah-mohs_

I didn't order this.	**Esto no es lo que pedí.** _ehs_-toh noh ehs loh keh peh-_dee_
I ordered…	**Pedí…** peh-_dee_…
I can't eat this.	**No puedo comerme esto.** noh _pweh_-doh koh-_mehr_-meh ehs-toh
This is too…	**Esto está demasiado…** ehs-toh ehs-_tah_ deh-mah-_seeyah_-doh…
cold/hot	**frío/caliente** _free_-oh/kah-_leeyehn_-teh
salty/spicy	**salado/picante** sah-_lah_-doh/pee-_kahn_-teh
tough/bland	**duro/soso** _doo_-roh/_soh_-soh
This isn't clean/fresh.	**Esto no está limpio/fresco.** ehs-toh noh ehs-_tah_ _leem_-peeyoh/_frehs_-koh

Paying

The check [bill], please.	**La cuenta, por favor.** lah _kwehn_-tah pohr fah-_bohr_
Separate checks [bills], please.	**Cuentas separadas, por favor.** _kwehn_-tahs seh-pah-_rah_-dahs pohr fah-_bohr_
It's all together.	**Póngalo todo junto.** _pohn_-gah-loh toh-doh _khoon_-toh
Is service included?	**¿Está incluido el servicio?** ehs-_tah_ een-kloo-_ee_-doh ehl sehr-_bee_-theeyoh
What's this amount for?	**¿De qué es esta cantidad?** deh keh ehs ehs-tah kahn-tee-_dahth_
I didn't have that.	**Yo no tomé eso. Tomé…** yoh noh toh-_meh_
I had…	eh-soh toh-_meh_…
Can I pay by credit card?	**¿Puedo pagar con tarjeta de crédito?** _pweh_-doh pah-_gahr_ kohn tahr-_kheh_-tah deh _kreh_-dee-toh
Can I have a receipt/an itemized bill?	**¿Podría darme un recibo/una cuenta detallada?** poh-_dree_-ah _dahr_-meh oon reh-_thee_-boh/oo-nah _kwehn_-tah deh-tah-_yah_-dah
That was delicious!	**¡Estuvo delicioso!** ehs-_too_-boh deh-lee-_theeyoh_-soh
I've already paid.	**Ya he pagado** yah eh pah-_gah_-doh

Restaurants are generally required to include service charges as part of the bill, so tipping isn't customary. If you wish to leave a tip for good service, just round up the bill to the nearest euro or two.

Meals & Cooking

Breakfast

el agua *ehl ah·gwah*	water
el café/el té… *ehl kah·feh/ehl teh…*	coffee/tea…
con azúcar *kohn ah·thoo·kahr*	with sugar
con edulcorante artificial *kohn eh·dool·koh·rahn·teh ahr·tee·fee·theeyahl*	with artificial sweetener
con leche *kohn leh·cheh*	with milk
descafeinado *dehs·kah·feyee·nah·doh*	decaf
solo *soh·loh*	black
los cereales (calientes/fríos) *lohs theh·reh·ah·lehs (kah·leeyehn·tehs/free·ohs)*	(cold/hot) cereal
los fiambres *lohs fee·ahm·brehs*	cold cuts [charcuterie]

El desayuno (breakfast) is usually served from 8:00 a.m. to 10:00 a.m. **La comida** (lunch), generally the largest meal of the day, is served from 2:00-4:00 p.m. **La cena** (dinner) is typically smaller and lighter than in the U.S. or U.K., and is usually served after 9:00 p.m. For a snack between meals, you can get **tapas** in smaller restaurants and some bars.

la harina de avena *lah ah·ree·nah deh ah·beh·nah*   oatmeal

el huevo... *ehl weh·boh...*   egg...

   duro/pasado por agua *doo·roh/ pah·sah·doh pohr ah·gwah*   hard-/soft-boiled

   frito *free·toh*   fried

   revuelto *reh·bwehl·toh*   scrambled

los huevos a la flamenca *lohs weh·bohs ah lah flah·mehn·kah*   baked eggs with tomato, onion and ham

la leche *lah leh·cheh*   milk

la magdalena *lah mahg·dah·leh·nah*   muffin

la mantequilla *lah mahn·teh·kee·yah*   butter

la mermelada/la jalea *lah mehr·meh·lah·dah/khah·leh·ah*   jam/jelly

el muesli *ehl mwehs·lee*   granola [muesli]

el pan *ehl pahn*   bread

el panecillo *ehl pah·neh·thee·yoh*   roll

el queso *ehl keh·soh*   cheese

la salchicha *lah sahl·chee·chah*   sausage

el tocino *ehl toh·thee·noh*   bacon

la tortilla... *lah tohr·tee·yah...*   omelet...

   de patatas *deh pah·tah·tahs*   with potato (and sometimes onion)

   de jamón *deh khah·mohn*   with ham

   paisana *payee·sah·nah*   with potatoes, peas and shrimp or ham

   de queso *deh keh·soh*   with cheese

   de setas *deh seh·tahs*   with mushrooms

la tostada *lah tohs·tah·dah*   toast

el yogur *ehl yoh·goor*   yogurt

el zumo de... *ehl thoo·moh deh...*   ...juice
  manzana *mahn·thah·nah*   apple
  pomelo *poh·meh·loh*   grapefruit
  naranja *nah·rahn·khah*   orange

Appetizers

las aceitunas (rellenas) *lahs ah·theyee·too·nahs (reh·yeh·nahs)*   (stuffed) olives

las albóndigas *lahs ahl·bohn·dee·gahs*   meatballs

el bacalao *ehl bah·kah·laoh*   dried salt cod

los boquerones en vinagre *lohs boh·keh·roh·nehs ehn bee·nah·greh*   anchovies marinated in garlic and olive oil

los callos *lohs kah·yohs*   tripe in hot paprika sauce

los caracoles *lohs kah·rah·koh·lehs*   snails

los champiñones al ajillo *lohs chahm·pee·nyoh·nehs ahl ah·khee·yoh*   mushrooms fried in olive oil with garlic

las croquetas *lahs kroh·keh·tahs*   croquettes with various fillings

las gambas al ajillo *lahs gahm·bahs ahl ah·khee·yoh*   broiled shrimp in garlic

el pan con tomate *ehl pahn kohn toh·mah·teh*   toasted bread with garlic, tomato and olive oil

los pescados fritos *lohs pehs·kah·dohs free·tohs*   fried fish

Tapas are snacks, similar to appetizers, served in cafés and bars. Many bars have their own specialties. When ordering, **una tapa** is a mouthful, **una ración** is half a plateful and **una porción** is a generous amount.

los pimientos *lohs pee·meeyehn·tohs*		peppers
los pinchos *lohs peen·chohs*		grilled, skewered meat
los quesos *lohs keh·sohs*		cheese platter
la tortilla española *lah tohr·tee·yah ehs·pah·nyoh·lah*		potato omelet

Soup

el caldo gallego *ehl kahl·doh gah·yeh·goh*	stew of cabbage, potatoes, beans and meat, from Galicia region
el cocido *ehl koh·thee·doh*	chickpea stew with potatoes, cabbage, turnips, beef, bacon, chorizo and black pudding
el consomé al jerez *ehl kohn·soh·meh ahl kheh·rehth*	chicken broth with sherry
la fabada asturiana *lah fah·bah·dah ahs·too·reeyah·nah*	white bean stew
el gazpacho *ehl gahth·pah·choh*	cold tomato soup
el marmitako *ehl mahr·mee·tah·koh*	tuna fish and potato stew, from the Basque region
la sopa... *lah soh·pah...*	...soup
castellana *kahs·teh·yah·nah*	with garlic, chunks of ham and a poached egg
de ajo blanco *deh ah·khoh blahn·koh*	with garlic and almond, served cold, popular in Andalucia
de habas *deh ah·bahs*	bean
de mariscos *deh mah·rees·kohs*	seafood
de pollo *deh poh·yoh*	chicken
de tomate *deh toh·mah·teh*	tomato
de verduras *deh behr·doo·rahs*	vegetable

Fish & Seafood

la almeja *lah ahl·meh·khah* — clam

el arenque *ehl ah·rehn·keh* — herring

el atún *ehl ah·toon* — tuna

el bacalao a la vizcaína *ehl bah·kah·laoh ah lah beeth·kayee·nah* — cod with dried peppers and onions

el bacalao *ehl bah·kah·laoh* — cod

el besugo *ehl beh·soo·goh* — sea bream

el boquerón *ehl boh·keh·rohn* — fresh baby anchovy

la caballa *lah kah·bah·yah* — mackerel

el calamar *ehl kah·lah·mahr* — squid

los calamares a la romana *lohs kah·lah·mahr·ehs ah lah roh·mah·nah* — deep-fried battered squid

el cangrejo *ehl kahn·greh·khoh* — crab

el chipirón *ehl chee·pee·rohn* — small whole squid

las cigalas *lahs thee·gah·lahs* — crayfish

las cigalas cocidas *lahs thee·gah·lahs koh·thee·dahs* — boiled crayfish

el fletán *ehl fleh·tahn* — halibut

la gamba *lah gahm·bah* — shrimp

las gambas en cerveza *lahs gahm·bahs ehn thehr·beh·thah* — shrimp in beer

la langosta *lah lahn·gohs·tah* — lobster

el lenguado *ehl lehn·gwah·doh* — sole

la lubina *lah loo·bee·nah* — sea bass

la mariscada *lah mah·rees·kah·dah* — cold mixed shellfish

los mejillones *lohs meh·khee·yoh·nehs* — mussels

los mejillones en escabeche *lohs meh·khee·yohn·ehs ehn ehs·kah·beh·cheh* — mussels in a marinade

la merluza *lah mehr·loo·thah* — hake

la merluza a la sidra *lah mehr·loo·thah*   hake in cider
ah lah see·drah

el mero *ehl meh·roh*   grouper

la ostra *lah ohs·trah*   oyster

el pez espada *ehl pehth ehs·pah·dah*   swordfish

el pulpo *ehl pool·poh*   octopus

el pulpo a la gallega *ehl pool·poh ah lah*   octopus with olive
gah·yeh·gah   oil and paprika

el salmón *ehl sahl·mohn*   salmon

el tiburón *ehl tee·boo·rohn*   shark

la trucha *lah troo·chah*   trout

la trucha a la navarra *lah troo·chah ah*   grilled trout stuffed
lah nah·bah·rrah   with ham

la zarzuela de pescado   mixed fish and seafood
lah thahr·thweh·lah deh pehs·kah·doh   cooked in broth,
   served over bread

Meat & Poultry

la asadurilla de cordero   lamb's liver
lah ah·sah·doo·rree·yah deh kohr·deh·roh

la butifarra *lah boo·tee·fah·rrah*   spiced pork sausage, popular
   in Cataluña and Valencia

los callos a la madrileña *lohs kah·yohs*   tripe stew, a Madrid
ah lah mah·dree·leh·nyah   specialty

la carne *lah kahr·neh*   meat

la carne de cerdo *lah kahr·neh deh thehr·doh*   pork

la carne picada *lah kahr·neh pee·kah·dah*   ground beef

la carne de vaca *lah kahr·neh deh bah·kah*   beef

el chorizo *ehl choh·ree·thoh*   highly-seasoned
   pork sausage

la chuleta *lah choo·leh·tah*   chop

el cochifrito navarro *ehl koh·chee·free·toh nah·bah·rroh* — deep-fried lamb pieces

el conejo *ehl koh·neh·khoh* — rabbit

el cordero *ehl kohr·deh·roh* — lamb

la cordorniz *lah kohr·dohr·neeth* — quail

las costillas de cerdo *lahs kohs·tee·yahs deh thehr·doh* — pork ribs

las empanadas *lahs ehm·pah·nah·dahs* — pastry filled with meat, chicken or tuna, a specialty of Galicia

los espárragos montañeses *lohs ehs·pah·rrah·gohs mohn·tah·nyeh·sehs* — calves's tails

la falda de buey *lah fahl·dah deh bwehy* — beef flank steak

el filete *ehl fee·leh·teh* — steak

las gallinejas *lahs gah·yee·neh·khahs* — fried lamb intestine

el guisado de riñones *ehl gee·sah·doh deh ree·nyoh·nehs* — kidney stew

el hígado *ehl ee·gah·doh* — liver

el jamón *ehl khah·mohn* — ham

el jamón ibérico *ehl khah·mohn ee·beh·ree·koh* — aged Iberian ham

el jamón serrano *ehl khah·mohn seh·rrah·noh* — dry-cured serrano ham

el lacón con grelos *ehl lah·kohn kohn greh·lohs* — salted ham with turnip greens, typical of Galicia

las magras con tomate *lahs mah·grahs kohn toh·mah·teh* — lightly fried ham dipped in tomato sauce

las manos de cerdo *lahs mah·nohs deh thehr·doh* — pig's feet [trotters]

las mollejas de ternera *lahs moh·yeh·khahs deh tehr·neh·rah* — veal sweetbread

la morcilla *lah mohr·thee·yah* — blood sausage
la paella… *lah pah·eh·yah…* — paella…
de carne *deh kahr·neh* — with chicken and sausage (may be made with beef)

de marisco *deh mah·rees·koh* — with seafood
de verduras *deh behr·doo·rahs* — with vegetables
valenciana *bah·lehn·theeyah·nah* — with chicken, shrimp, mussels, squid, peas, tomato, garlic, olive oil, paprika; from the Valencia region

zamorana *thah·moh·rah·nah* — with ham, pork loin, pig's feet; popular in the Zamora region

las patatas con chorizo *lahs pah·tah·tahs kohn choh·ree·thoh* — potatoes with chorizo sausage
el pato *ehl pah·toh* — duck
el pavo *ehl pah·boh* — turkey
el pollo *ehl poh·yoh* — chicken
el pollo frito *ehl poh·yoh free·toh* — fried chicken
el riñón *ehl ree·nyohn* — kidney
la salchicha *lah sahl·chee·chah* — sausage
el salchichón *ehl sahl·chee·chohn* — salami-type sausage
el solomillo *ehl soh·loh·mee·yoh* — filet mignon
la ternera *lah tehr·neh·rah* — veal
el tocino *ehl toh·thee·noh* — bacon
la trucha a la navarra *lah troo·chah ah lah nah·bah·rrah* — trout fried with a piece of ham
el venado *ehl beh·nah·doh* — venison

Paella is a specialty dish of Spain. Traditional **paella**, which originated in Valencia, includes rice, saffron, vegetables, rabbit and chicken. **Paella de marisco** (seafood **paella**) is a very popular version of this dish, especially along the coast. Other delicious versions are noted above.

Vegetables & Staples

la aceituna *lah ah•theyee•too•nah*	olive
la acelga *lah ah•thehl•gah*	chard
el aguacate *ehl ah•gwah•khah•teh*	avocado
el ajo *ehl ah•khoh*	garlic
la albahaca *lah ahl•bah•ah•kah*	basil
la alcachofa (salteada) *lah ahl•kah•choh•fah (sahl•teh•ah•dah)*	(sauteed) artichoke
la alcaparra *lah ahl•kah•pah•rrah*	caper
el anís *ehl ah•nees*	aniseed
el apio *ehl ah•peeyoh*	celery
el arroz... *ehl ah•rrohth...*	rice...
con habas y nabos *kohn ah•bahs ee nah•bohs*	with beans and turnips
a la cubana *ah lah koo•bah•nah*	with fried eggs and banana fritters
empedrado *ehm•peh•drah•doh*	with tomatoes and cod and a top layer of white beans
santanderino *sahn• tahn•deh•ree•noh*	with salmon and milk
el azafrán *ehl ah•thah•frahn*	saffron
los bajoques farcides *lohs bah•khoh•kehs fahr•thee•dehs*	red peppers stuffed with rice, pork and tomatoes; from Catalonia

la batata *lah bah·tah·tah* — yam

la berenjena *lah beh·rehn·kheh·nah* — eggplant [aubergine]

el brécol *ehl breh·kohl* — broccoli

los brotes de soja *lohs broh·tehs deh soh·khah* — bean sprouts

el calabacín *ehl kah·lah·bah·theen* — zucchini [courgette]

la cassolada *lah kahs·soh·lah·dah* — rice casserole with thrushes (a type of bird) and ribs, from Catalonia

la cebolla *lah theh·boh·yah* — onion

el champiñon (a la plancha/salteado) *ehl chahm·pee·nyohn (ah lah plahn·chah/sahl·teh·ah·doh)* — (grilled/sautéed) mushroom

la coliflor *lah koh·lee·flohr* — cauliflower

el espárrago *ehl ehs·pah·rrah·goh* — asparagus

la espinaca *lah ehs·pee·nah·kah* — spinach

la faba *lah fah·bah* — white bean

el guisante *ehl gee·sahn·teh* — pea

las habas a la catalana *lahs ah·bahs a lah kah·tah·lah·nah* — broad bean

la harina *lah ah·ree·nah* — flour

la judía *lah khoo·dee·ah* — bean

la judía verde *lah khoo·dee·ah behr·deh* — green bean

la lechuga *lah leh·choo·gah* — lettuce

la lenteja *lah lehn·teh·khah* — lentil

el maíz *ehl mah·eeth* — corn

la menestra *lah meh·nehs·trah* — vegetable stew

las migas de pastor *lahs mee·gahs deh pahs·tohr* — bread soaked in water then fried with pieces of bacon and dried peppers

el pan *ehl pahn* — bread

la pasta *lah pahs·tah*	pasta
la patata *lah pah·tah·tah*	potato
el pepino *ehl peh·pee·noh*	cucumber
el perejil *ehl peh·reh·kheel*	parsley
el pimiento relleno *ehl pee·meeyehn·toh reh·yeh·noh*	stuffed pepper
el pimiento rojo/verde *ehl pee·meeyehn·toh roh·khoh/behr·deh*	red/green pepper
el repollo *ehl reh·poh·yoh*	cabbage
la seta *lah seh·tah*	mushroom
el tomate *ehl toh·mah·teh*	tomato
la verdura *lah behr·doo·rah*	vegetable
la zanahoria *lah thah·nah·oh·reeyah*	carrot

Fruit

el albaricoque *ehl ahl·bah·ree·koh·keh*	apricot
el arándano *ehl ah·rahn·dah·noh*	blueberry
el arándano rojo *ehl ah·rahn·dah·noh roh·khoh*	cranberry
la cereza *lah theh·reh·thah*	cherry
la ciruela *lah thee·rweh·lah*	plum
el coco *ehl koh·koh*	coconut
la frambuesa *lah frahm·bweh·sah*	raspberry
la fresa *lah freh·sah*	strawberry
la fruta *lah froo·tah*	fruit
la guayaba *lah gwah·yah·bah*	guava
el kiwi *ehl kee·wee*	kiwi
la lima *lah lee·mah*	lime
el limón *ehl lee·mohn*	lemon
la mandarina *lah mahn·dah·ree·nah*	tangerine
el mango *ehl mahn·goh*	mango
la manzana *lah mahn·thah·nah*	apple

el melocotón *ehl meh·loh·koh·tohn*   peach
el melón *ehl meh·lohn*   melon
la naranja *lah nah·rahn·khah*   orange
la papaya *lah pah·pah·yah*   papaya
la pera *lah peh·rah*   pear
la piña *lah pee·nyah*   pineapple
el plátano *ehl plah·tah·noh*   banana
el pomelo *ehl poh·meh·loh*   grapefruit
la sandía *lah sahn·dee·ah*   watermelon
la uva *lah oo·bah*   grape

Cheese

el queso… *ehl keh·soh…*   …cheese
  blando *blahn·doh*   soft, mild-flavored
  de Burgos *deh boor·gohs*   soft, creamy regional variety
  Cabrales *kah·brah·lehs*   tangy, blue-veined regional variety

  cremoso *kreh·moh·soh*   cream
  curado *koo·rah·doh*   ripe
  de leche de cabra *deh leh·cheh deh kah·brah*   from goat's milk
  duro *doo·roh*   hard
  fuerte *fwehr·teh*   strong
  Manchego *mahn·cheh·goh*   hard cheese from Manchego sheep's milk

  Perilla *peh·ree·yah*   firm, bland regional variety
  rallado *rah·yah·doh*   grated
  requesón *reh·keh·sohn*   cottage
  Roncal *rohn·kahl*   sharp goat cheese, salted and smoked, regional variety

  suave *swah·beh*   mild
  tipo roquefort *tee·poh roh·qeh·fohrt*   blue

Dessert

el arroz con leche *ehl ah·rroth kohn leh·cheh*	rice pudding
el brazo de gitano *ehl brah·thoh deh khee·tah·noh*	sponge cake roll with cream filling
el buñuelo *ehl boo·nyweh·loh*	thin, deep-fried fritter, covered in sugar
el canutillo *ehl kah·noo·tee·yoh*	custard pastry horn with cinnamon
el churro *ehl choo·rroh*	deep-fried fritter sprinkled with sugar
la filloa *lah fee·yoh·ah*	crepe (used in sweet or savory dishes), typical of Galicia region
el flan *ehl flahn*	caramel custard
la galleta *lah gah·yeh·tah*	cookie [biscuit]
el helado *ehl eh·lah·doh*	ice cream
la leche frita *lah leh·cheh free·tah*	fried milk custard
la mantecada *lah mahn·teh·kah·dah*	small sponge cake
la manzana asada *lah mahn·thah·nah ah·sah·dah*	baked apple
el pastel de queso *ehl pahs·tehl deh keh·soh*	cheesecake
el sorbete *ehl sohr·beh·teh*	sorbet
la tarta de Santiago *lah tahr·tah deh sahn·teeyah·goh*	dense almond cake topped with powdered sugar
el tocino de cielo *ehl toh·thee·noh deh theeyeh·loh*	egg yolk custard

Sauces & Condiments

salt	**la sal** *lah sahl*
black pepper	**la pimienta negra** *lah pee·meeyehn·tah neh·grah*
mustard	**mostaza** *mohs·tah·thah*

| ketchup | **ketchup** keht•choop |
| sugar | **el azúcar** ehl ah•thoo•kahr |

At the Market

Where are the carts [trolleys]/baskets?	**¿Dónde están los carritos/las cestas?** dohn•deh ehs•tahn lohs kah•rree•tohs/lahs thehs•tahs
Where is …?	**¿Donde está…?** dohn•deh ehs•tah…
I'd like some of that/this.	**Quiero un poco de eso/esto.** keeyeh•roh oon poh•koh deh eh•soh/ehs•toh
Can I taste it?	**¿Puedo probarlo?** pweh•doh proh•bahr•loh
I'd like…	**Quiero…** keeyeh•roh…
a kilo/half-kilo of…	**un kilo/medio kilo de…** oon kee•loh/ meh•deeyoh kee•loh deh…
a liter of…	**un litro de…** oon lee•troh deh…
a piece of…	**un trozo de…** oon troh•thoh deh…
a slice of…	**una rodaja de…** oo•nah roh•dah•khah deh…
More/Less.	**Más/Menos.** mahs/meh•nohs
How much?	**¿Cuánto es?** kwahn•toh ehs
Where do I pay?	**¿Dónde se paga?** dohn•deh seh pah•gah
A bag, please.	**Una bolsa, por favor.** oo•nah bohl•sah pohr fah•bohr
I'm being helped.	**Ya me atienden.** yah meh ah•teeyehn•dehn

YOU MAY HEAR...

¿Necesita ayuda?	Can I help you?
neh·theh·see·tah ah·yoo·dah	
¿Qué desea? *keh deh·seh·ah*	What would you like?
¿Algo más? *ahl·goh mahs*	Anything else?
Son...euros. *sohn...ew·rohs*	That's...euros.

In Spain, food is often purchased at local family-run markets. These are excellent places for regional and specialty foods, fresh fruit and vegetables, meat and baked goods. **Hipermercados** (large grocery store chains) are also common, but these are usually found on the outskirts of town or in the suburbs. These stores have a larger selection than regular supermarkets, and are often less expensive. **Alcampo**, **Carrefour** and **Hipercor** are common chains. **El Corte Inglés** is a popular department store chain that has a supermarket on the ground floor in some locations, but it tends to have higher prices than regular supermarkets.

In the Kitchen

bottle opener	**el abrebotellas**	*ehl ah·breh·boh·teh·yahs*
bowl	**el cuenco**	*ehl kwehn·koh*
can opener	**el abrelatas**	*ehl ah·breh·lah·tahs*
corkscrew	**el sacacorchos**	*ehl sah·kah·kohr·chohs*
cup	**la taza**	*lah tah·thah*
fork	**el tenedor**	*ehl teh·neh·dohr*
frying pan	**la sartén**	*lah sahr·tehn*

Measurements in Europe are metric - and that applies to the weight of food too. If you tend to think in pounds and ounces, it's worth brushing up on what the metric equivalent is before you go shopping for fruit and veg in markets and supermarkets. Five hundred grams, or half a kilo, is a common quantity to order, and that converts to just over a pound (17.65 ounces, to be precise).

glass	**el vaso** *ehl bah•soh*
(steak) knife	**el cuchillo (de carne)** *ehl koo•chee•yoh (deh kahr•neh)*
measuring cup/spoon	**la taza/la cuchara medidora** *lah tah•thah/ lah koo•chah•rah meh•dee•doh•rah*
napkin	**la servilleta** *lah sehr•bee•yeh•tah*
plate	**el plato** *ehl plah•toh*
pot	**la olla** *lah oh•yah*
saucepan	**el cazo** *ehl kah•thoh*
spatula	**la espátula** *lah ehs•pah•too•lah*
spoon	**la cuchara** *lah koo•chah•rah*

YOU MAY SEE...

CONSUMIR PREFERENTEMENTE ANTES DE...	best if used by...
CALORÍAS	calories
SIN GRASA	fat free
CONSERVAR EN FRIGORÍFICO	keep refrigerated
PUEDE CONTENER TRAZAS DE...	may contain traces of...
FECHA LÍMITE DE VENTA...	sell by...
APTO PARA VEGETARIANOS	suitable for vegetarians

Drinks

ESSENTIAL

Can I see the wine list/ drink menu, please?	**La carta de vinos/bebidas, por favor.** *lah kahr·tah deh bee·nohs/beh·bee·dahs pohr fah·bohr*
What do you recommend?	**¿Qué me recomienda?** *keh meh reh·koh·meeyehn·dah*
I'd like a bottle/glass of red/white wine.	**Quiero una botella/un vaso de vino tinto/blanco.** *keeyeh·roh oo·nah boh·teh·yah/ oon bah·soh deh bee·noh teen·toh/blahn·koh*
The house wine, please.	**El vino de la casa, por favor.** *ehl bee·noh deh lah kah·sah pohr fah·bohr*
Another bottle/glass, please.	**Otra botella/Otro vaso, por favor.** *oh·trah boh·teh·yah/oh·troh bah·soh pohr fah·bohr*
I'd like a local beer.	**Quiero una cerveza española.** *keeyeh·roh oo·nah thehr·beh·thah ehs·pah·nyoh·lah*
Can I buy you a drink?	**¿Puedo invitarle m /invitarla f a una copa?** *pweh·doh een·bee·tahr·leh/ een·bee·tahr·lah ah oo·nah koh·pah*
Cheers!	**¡Salud!** *sah·looth*
A coffee/tea, please.	**Un café/té, por favor.** *oon kah·feh/teh pohr fah·bohr*
Black.	**Solo.** *soh·loh*
With...	**Con...** *kohn...*
milk	**leche** *leh·cheh*
sugar	**azúcar** *ah·thoo·kahr*
artificial sweetener	**edulcorante artificial** *eh·dool·khoh·rahn·teh ahr·tee·fee·theeyahl*
A..., please.	**Un..., por favor.** *oon...pohr fah·bohr*
juice	**zumo** *thoo·moh*
soda	**refresco** *reh·frehs·koh*

water	**agua** _ah·gwah_
sparkling/still	**con/sin gas** _kohn/seen gahs_
Is the tap water	**¿Se puede beber el agua del grifo?**
safe to drink?	_seh pweh·deh beh·behr ehl ah·gwah dehl gree·foh_

Non-alcoholic Drinks

el agua (con/sin gas) _ehl ah·gwah_ _(kohn/seen gahs)_	(sparkling/still) water
el café _ehl kah·feh_	coffee
el chocolate caliente _ehl choh·koh·lah·teh kah·leeyehn·teh_	hot chocolate
el granizado _ehl grah·nee·thah·doh_	iced drink
la horchata _lah ohr·chah·tah_	sweet drink made from tiger nuts and sugar
la leche _lah leh·cheh_	milk
la limonada _lah lee·moh·nah·dah_	lemonade
el refresco _ehl reh·frehs·koh_	soda
el té (con hielo) _ehl teh (kohn eeyeh·loh)_	(iced) tea
el zumo _ehl thoo·moh_	juice

Aperitifs, Cocktails & Liqueurs

el coñac _ehl koh·nyahk_	brandy
la ginebra _lah khee·neh·brah_	gin
el jerez fino _ehl kheh·rehth fee·noh_	pale, dry sherry
el jerez oloroso _ehl kheh·rehth oh·loh·roh·soh_	dark, heavy sherry
el licor _ehl lee·kohr_	liqueur
el oporto _ehl oh·pohr·toh_	port
el ron _ehl rohn_	rum
la sangría _lah sahn·gree·ah_	wine punch
el tequila _ehl teh·kee·lah_	tequila

YOU MAY HEAR...

¿Qué desea beber? *keh deh•seh•ah beh•behr* Can I get you a drink?

¿Con leche o azúcar? With milk or sugar?
kohn leh•cheh oh ah•thoo•kahr

¿Agua con gas o sin gas? Sparkling or still
ah•gwah kohn gahs oh seen gahs water?

el vodka *ehl bohd•kah*	vodka
el whisky *ehl wees•kee*	whisky
el whisky escocés *ehl wees•kee ehs•koh•thehs*	scotch

Beer

la cerveza... *lah thehr•beh•thah...*	...beer
en botella/de barril *ehn boh•teh•yah/ deh bah•rreel*	bottled/draft
española/extranjera *ehs•pah•nyoh•lah/ ehx•trahn•kheh•rah*	local/imported
negra/ligera *neh•grah/lee•kheh•rah*	dark/light
rubia/pilsner *roo•beeyah/peels•nehr*	lager/pilsner
sin alcohol *seen ahl•koh•ohl*	non-alcoholic

Many Spaniards love coffee and drink it throughout the day.
Bottled water is available, though tap water is used in the home
and is generally safe to drink. Restaurants will almost always serve
bottled water with meals, unless you specifically request **agua del
grifo** (tap water). Juice is usually served with breakfast, but it's not
common at lunch or dinner.

There are many popular brands of beer in Spain, including **San Miguel®, Cruzcampo®, Alhambra®, Mahou®, Estrella Damm®** and **Zaragozana®**. Each brand usually has several classes and types of beer available, though most will be a lager-type beer. The classes of beer include **clásica**, a light, pale, pilsner-type lager; **especial**, a heavier pilsner-type lager; **negra**, a dark, malty lager; and **extra**, a heavy, high-alcohol lager.

Wine

el cava ehl _kah_·bah	sparkling wine
el champán ehl chahm·_pahn_	champagne
el vino... ehl _bee_·noh...	...wine
de la casa/de mesa deh lah _kah_·sah/ deh _meh_·sah	house/table
espumoso ehs·poo·_moh_·soh	sparkling
tinto/blanco _teen_·toh/_blahn_·koh	red/white
seco/dulce _seh_·koh/_dool_·theh	dry/sweet

With 40 recognized wine regions, Spain has the largest land area under vine in the world and is the third largest producer and exporter of wine. The most well-known types of wine include red wine from Rioja and Ribera del Duero, sherries from Jerez, white wine from Rueda and red wine and white wine from Penedés. Another popular wine, especially in the summer time, is the sparkling white known as **cava**. Spanish wineries are known as **bodegas**; the winemaker is known as a **bodeguero**.

On the Menu

el aceite *ehl ah-theyee-teh* — oil

el aceite de oliva *ehl ah-theyee-teh deh oh-lee-bah* — olive oil

la aceituna *lah ah-theyee-too-nah* — olive

la acelga *lah ah-thehl-gah* — chard

la achicoria *lah ah-chee-koh-reeyah* — chicory

el agua *ehl ah-gwah* — water

el aguacate *ehl ah-gwah-kah-teh* — avocado

el ajo *ehl ah-khoh* — garlic

el ajo chalote *ehl ah-khoh chah-loh-teh* — shallot

la albahaca *lah ahl-bah-ah-kah* — basil

el albaricoque *ehl ahl-bah-ree-koh-keh* — apricot

la albóndiga *lah ahl-bohn-dee-gah* — meatball

la alcachofa *lah ahl-kah-choh-fah* — artichoke

la alcaparra *lah ahl-kah-pah-rrah* — caper

la alcaravea *lah ahl-kah-rah-beh-ah* — caraway

la almeja *lah ahl-meh-khah* — clam

la almendra *lah ahl-mehn-drah* — almond

el almíbar *ehl ahl-mee-bahr* — syrup

el anacardo *ehl ah-nah-kahr-doh* — cashew

las ancas de rana *lahs ahn-kahs deh rah-nah* — frog's legs

la anchoa *lah ahn-choh-ah* — anchovy

la anguila *lah ahn-gee-lah* — eel

la angula *lah ahn-goo-lah* — baby eel

el anís *ehl ah-nees* — aniseed

el aperitivo *ehl ah-peh-ree-tee-boh* — aperitif

el apio *ehl ah-peeyoh* — celery

el arándano *ehl ah-rahn-dah-noh* — blueberry

el arándano rojo *ehl ah-rahn-dah-noh roh-khoh* — cranberry

el arenque *ehl ah•rehn•keh*		herring
el arroz *ehl ah•rrohth*		rice
el arroz integral *ehl ah•rrohth een•teh•grahl*		whole grain rice
el arroz salvaje *ehl ah•rrohth sahl•bah•kheh*		wild rice
el asado *ehl ah•sah•doh*		roast
las asaduras *lahs ah•sah•doo•rahs*		organ meat [offal]
el atún *ehl ah•toon*		tuna
la avellana *lah ah•beh•yah•nah*		hazelnut
la avena *lah ah•beh•nah*		oat
las aves *lahs ah•behs*		poultry
el azafrán *ehl ah•thah•frahn*		saffron
el azúcar *ehl ah•thoo•kahr*		sugar
el bacalao *bah•kah•lao*		cod
los barquillos *lohs bahr•kee•yohs*		wafers/ice cream cones
la batata *lah bah•tah•tah*		sweet potato
el batido *ehl bah•tee•doh*		milk shake
la bebida *lah beh•bee•dah*		drink
la berenjena *lah beh•rehn•kheh•nah*		eggplant [aubergine]
la berraza *lah beh•rrah•thah*		parsnip
el berro *ehl beh•rroh*		watercress
la berza *lah behr•thah*		kale
el besugo *ehl beh•soo•goh*		sea bream
blando *blahn•doh*		soft
el bollo *ehl boh•yoh*		pastry
el brandy *ehl brahn•dee*		brandy
el brécol *ehl breh•kohl*		broccoli
los brotes de soja *lohs broh•tehs deh soh•khah*		bean sprouts
el buey *ehl bwehy*		ox
el buñuelo *ehl boo•nyweh•loh*		fritter
la caballa *lah kah•bah•yah*		mackerel
la cabra *lah kah•brah*		goat

el cabrito *ehl kah-bree-toh*	young goat
el cacahuete *ehl kah-kah-weh-teh*	peanut
el café *ehl kah-feh*	coffee
el café solo *ehl kah-feh soh-loh*	espresso
el calabacín *ehl kah-lah-bah-theen*	zucchini [courgette]
la calabaza *lah kah-lah-bah-thah*	pumpkin
el calamar *ehl kah-lah-mahr*	squid
el caldo *ehl kahl-doh*	broth
los callos *lohs kah-yohs*	tripe
la canela *lah kah-neh-lah*	cinnamon
el cangrejo *ehl kahn-greh-khoh*	crab
el capuchino *ehl kah-poo-chee-noh*	cappuccino
el caracol *ehl kah-rah-kohl*	snail
el caramelo *ehl kah-rah-meh-loh*	candy [sweet]
la carne *lah kahr-neh*	meat
la carne de cangrejo *lah kahr-neh deh kahn-greh-khoh*	crabmeat
la carne de cerdo *lah kahr-neh deh thehr-doh*	pork
la carne picada *lah kahr-neh pee-kah-dah*	ground beef
la carne de vaca *lah kahr-neh deh bah-kah*	beef
el carnero *ehl kahr-neh-roh*	mutton

las carrilladas *lahs kah·rree·yah·dahs*	cow's cheeks
casero *kah·seh·roh*	homemade
la castaña *lah kahs·tah·nyah*	chestnut
el cava *ehl kah·bah*	sparkling wine
la caza *lah kah·thah*	game
la cebolla *lah theh·boh·yah*	onion
la cebolleta *lah theh·boh·yeh·tah*	scallion [spring onion]
los cebollinos *lohs theh·boh·yee·nohs*	chives
la cecina de bovino *lah theh·thee·nah deh boh·bee·noh*	corned beef
el centeno *ehl thehn·teh·noh*	rye
el centollo *ehl thehn·toh·yoh*	spider crab
el cereal *ehl theh·reh·ahl*	cereal
la cereza *lah theh·reh·thah*	cherry
la cerveza *lah thehr·beh·thah*	beer
el champiñón *ehl chahm·pee·nyohn*	mushroom
el champán *ehl chahm·pahn*	champagne
la chirivía *lah chee·ree·bee·ah*	parsnip
el chipirón *ehl chee·pee·rohn*	small whole squid
el chocolate *ehl choh·koh·lah·teh*	chocolate
el chocolate caliente *ehl choh·koh·lah·teh kah·leeyehn·teh*	hot chocolate
el chorizo *ehl choh·ree·thoh*	highly-seasoned pork sausage
la chuleta *lah choo·leh·tah*	chop
el chuletón *ehl choo·leh·tohn*	T-bone steak
el ciervo *ehl theeyehr·boh*	deer
la cigala *lah thee·gah·lah*	crayfish
el cilantro *ehl thee·lahn·troh*	cilantro [coriander]
la ciruela *lah thee·rweh·lah*	plum
la ciruela pasa *lah thee·rweh·lah pah·sah*	prune

el clavo *ehl klah·boh* — clove

el cochinillo *ehl koh·chee·nee·yoh* — suckling pig

el coco *ehl koh·koh* — coconut

la codorniz *lah koh·dohr·neeth* — quail

la col *lah kohl* — cabbage

las coles de Bruselas *lahs koh·lehs deh broo·seh·lahs* — Brussels sprouts

la coliflor *lah koh·lee·flohr* — cauliflower

el comino *ehl koh·mee·noh* — cumin

la compota *lah kohm·poh·tah* — stewed fruit

con alcohol *kohn ahl·koh·ohl* — with alcohol

con nata *kohn nah·tah* — with cream

el condimento *ehl kohn·dee·mehn·toh* — relish

el conejo *ehl koh·neh·khoh* — rabbit

el congrio *ehl kohn·greeyoh* — conger eel

el consomé *ehl kohn·soh·meh* — consommé

el coñac *ehl koh·nyahk* — brandy

el corazón *ehl koh·rah·thohn* — heart

el cordero *ehl kohr·deh·roh* — lamb

la cordorniz *lah kohr·dohr·neeth* — quail

el coriandro *ehl koh·reeyahn·droh* — coriander

la croqueta *lah kroh·keh·tah* — croquette

el cruasán *ehl krwah·sahn* — croissant

crudo *kroo·doh* — raw

los dátiles *lohs dah·tee·lehs* — dates

descafeinado *dehs·kah·feyey·nah·doh* — decaffeinated

el edulcorante artificial *ehl eh·dool·koh·rahn·teh ahr·tee·fee·theeyahl* — artificial sweetener

la empanada *lah ehm·pah·nah·dah* — pastry filled with meat, chicken, tuna or vegetables

el encurtido *ehl ehn·koor·tee·doh* — pickled

la endibia *lah ehn·dee·beeyah* — endive

el eneldo *ehl eh·nehl·doh* — dill

la ensalada *lah ehn·sah·lah·dah* — salad

la escarola *lah ehs·kah·roh·lah* — escarole [chicory]

el espagueti *ehl ehs·pah·geh·tee* — spaghetti

la espaldilla *lah ehs·pahl·dee·yah* — shoulder

el espárrago *ehl ehs·pah·rrah·goh* — asparagus

las especias *lahs ehs·peh·theeyahs* — spices

la espinaca *lah ehs·pee·nah·kah* — spinach

el estragón *ehl ehs·trah·gohn* — tarragon

el faisán *ehl fayee·sahn* — pheasant

la falda de ternera *lah fahl·dah deh tehr·neh·rah* — beef brisket

los fiambres *lohs feeyahm·brehs* — cold cuts [charcuterie]

el fideo *ehl fee·deh·oh* — noodle

el filete *ehl fee·leh·teh* — steak

el flan *ehl flahn* — caramel custard

el fletán *ehl fleh·tahn* — halibut

la frambuesa *lah frahm·bweh·sah* — raspberry

la fresa *lah freh·sah* — strawberry

la fruta *lah froo·tah* — fruit

los frutos secos *lohs froo·tohs seh·kohs* — nuts

la galleta *lah gah·yeh·tah* — cookie [biscuit]

la galleta salada *lah gah·yeh·tah sah·lah·dah* — cracker

la gamba *lah gahm·bah* — shrimp

el ganso *ehl gahn·soh* — wild goose

el garbanzo *ehl gahr·bahn·thoh* — chickpea

el gazpacho *ehl gahth·pah·choh* — cold tomato-based soup

la ginebra *lah khee·neh·brah* — gin

el gofre *ehl goh·freh* — waffle

la granada *lah grah·nah·dah* — pomegranate

el granizado *ehl grah·nee·thah·doh* — iced drink

la grosella espinosa *lah groh·seh·yah ehs·pee·noh·sah* — gooseberry

la grosella negra *lah groh·seh·yah neh·grah* — black currant

la grosella roja *lah groh·seh·yah roh·khah* — red currant

la guayaba *lah gwah·yah·bah* — guava

la guinda *lah geen·dah* — sour cherry

la guindilla en polvo *lah geen·dee·yah ehn pohl·boh* — chili pepper

el guirlache *ehl geer·lah·cheh* — nougat

el guisante *ehl gee·sahn·teh* — pea

la hamburguesa *lah ahm·boor·geh·sah* — hamburger

la harina *lah ah·ree·nah* — flour

la harina de avena *lah ah·ree·nah deh ah·beh·nah* — oatmeal

la harina de maíz *lah ah·ree·nah deh mah·eeth* — cornmeal

el helado *ehl eh·lah·doh* — ice cream

el (cubito de) hielo *ehl (koo·bee·toh deh) eeyeh·loh* — ice (cube)

el hígado *ehl ee·gah·doh*	liver
el higo *ehl ee·goh*	fig
el hinojo *ehl ee·noh·khoh*	fennel
la hoja de laurel *lah oh·khah deh lawoo·rehl*	bay leaf
el hueso *ehl weh·soh*	bone
el huevo *ehl weh·boh*	egg
el jabalí *ehl khah·bah·lee*	wild boar
la jalea *lah khah·leh·ah*	jelly
el jamón *ehl khah·mohn*	ham
el jengibre *ehl khehn·khee·breh*	ginger
el jerez *ehl kheh·rehth*	sherry
la judía *lah khoo·dee·ah*	bean
la judía verde *lah khoo·dee·ah behr·deh*	green bean
el ketchup *ehl keht·choop*	ketchup
el kiwi *ehl kee·wee*	kiwi
el lacón *ehl lah·kohn*	pork shoulder
la langosta *lah lahn·gohs·tah*	lobster
el lavanco *ehl lah·bahn·koh*	wild duck
la leche *lah leh·cheh*	milk
la leche de soja *lah leh·cheh deh soh·khah*	soymilk [soya milk]
la lechuga *lah leh·choo·gah*	lettuce
la lengua *lah lehn·gwah*	tongue
el lenguado *ehl lehn·gwah·doh*	sole
la lenteja *lah lehn·teh·khah*	lentil
el licor *ehl lee·kohr*	liqueur
el licor de naranja *ehl lee·kohr deh nah·rahn·khah*	orange liqueur
los licores *lohs lee·kohr·ehs*	spirits
la liebre *lah leyee·breh*	hare
la lima *lah lee·mah*	lime
el limón *ehl lee·mohn*	lemon

la limonada *lah leeh·moh·<u>nah</u>·dah* — lemonade

la lombarda *lah lohm·<u>bahr</u>·dah* — red cabbage

el lomo *ehl <u>loh</u>·moh* — loin

la lubina *lah loo·<u>bee</u>·nah* — (sea) bass

los macarrones *lohs mah·kah·<u>rrohn</u>·ehs* — macaroni

la magdalena *lah mahg·dah·<u>leh</u>·nah* — muffin

la maicena *lah mayee·<u>theh</u>·nah* — cornmeal

el maíz *ehl mah·<u>eeth</u>* — sweet corn

la mandarina *lah mahn·dah·<u>ree</u>·nah* — tangerine

el mango *ehl <u>mahn</u>·goh* — mango

las manos de cerdo *lahs <u>mah</u>·nohs deh <u>thehr</u>·doh* — pig's feet [trotters]

la mantequilla *lah mahn·teh·<u>kee</u>·yah* — butter

la manzana *lah mahn·<u>thah</u>·nah* — apple

la margarina *lah mahr·gah·<u>ree</u>·nah* — margarine

el marisco *ehl mah·<u>rees</u>·koh* — shellfish

la mayonesa *lah mah·yoh·<u>neh</u>·sah* — mayonnaise

el mazapán *ehl mah·thah·<u>pahn</u>* — marzipan

el mejillón *ehl meh·khee·<u>yohn</u>* — mussel

la mejorana *lah meh·khoh·<u>rah</u>·nah* — marjoram

la melaza *lah meh·<u>lah</u>·thah* — molasses

el melocotón *ehl meh·loh·koh·<u>tohn</u>* — peach

el melón *ehl meh·<u>lohn</u>* — melon

la menta *lah <u>mehn</u>·tah* — mint

el menudillo *ehl meh·noo·<u>dee</u>·yoh* — giblet

el merengue *ehl meh·<u>rehn</u>·geh* — meringue

la merluza *lah mehr·<u>loo</u>·thah* — hake

la mermelada *lah mehr·meh·<u>lah</u>·dah* — marmalade/jam

el mero *ehl <u>meh</u>·roh* — grouper

la miel *lah meeyehl* — honey

la molleja *lah moh·<u>yeh</u>·khah* — sweetbread

la morcilla *lah mohr•thee•yah*	black pudding
la mostaza *lah mohs•tah•thah*	mustard
el muesli *ehl mwehs•lee*	granola [muesli]
el nabo *ehl nah•boh*	turnip
la naranja *lah nah•rahn•khah*	orange
la nata *lah nah•tah*	cream
la nata agria *lah nah•tah ah•greeyah*	sour cream
la nata montada *lah nah•tah mohn•tah•dah*	whipped cream
las natillas *lahs nah•tee•yahs*	custard
la nuez *lah nwehth*	walnut
la nuez moscada *lah nwehth mohs•kah•dah*	nutmeg
el oporto *ehl oh•pohr•toh*	port
el orégano *ehl oh•reh•gah•noh*	oregano
la ostra *lah ohs•trah*	oyster
la pacana *lah pah•kah•nah*	pecan
la paella *lah pah•eh•yah*	rice dish
la paletilla *lah pah•leh•tee•yah*	shank
el palmito *ehl pahl•mee•toh*	palm heart
el pan *ehl pahn*	bread
el panecillo *ehl pah•neh•thee•yoh*	roll
la papaya *lah pah•pah•yah*	papaya
la paprika *lah pah•pree•kah*	paprika
la pasa *lah pah•sah*	raisin
la pasta *lah pahs•tah*	pasta
el pastel *ehl pahs•tehl*	pie
el pastel de queso *ehl pahs•tehl deh keh•soh*	cheesecake
la pata *lah pah•tah*	leg
la patata *lah pah•tah•tah*	potato
las patatas fritas *lahs pah•tah•tahs free•tahs*	French fries
las patatas fritas *lahs pah•tah•tahs free•tahs*	potato chips [crisps]
el paté *ehl pah•teh*	pâté

el pato *ehl pah·toh* — duck

el pavo *ehl pah·boh* — turkey

la pechuga (de pollo) *lah peh·choo·gah (deh poh·yoh)* — breast (of chicken)

el pepinillo *ehl peh·pee·nee·yoh* — pickle

el pepino *ehl peh·pee·noh* — cucumber

la pera *lah peh·rah* — pear

la perca *lah pehr·kah* — sea perch

la perdiz *lah pehr·deeth* — partridge

el perejil *ehl peh·reh·kheel* — parsley

el perrito caliente *ehl peh·rree·toh kah·leeyehn·teh* — hot dog

el pescadito *ehl pehs·kah·dee·toh* — small fish

el pescado *ehl pehs·kah·doh* — fish

el pescado frito *ehl pehs·kah·doh free·toh* — fried fish

pescado y marisco *pehs·kah·doh ee mah·rees·koh* — seafood

el pez espada *ehl peth ehs·pah·dah* — swordfish

el pichón *ehl pee·chohn* — young pigeon

pilsner *peels·nehr* — pilsner (beer)

el pimentón *ehl pee·mehn·tohn* — paprika

la pimienta *lah pee·meeyehn·tah* — pepper (seasoning)

la pimienta negra *lah pee·meeyehn·tah neh·grah* — black pepper

la pimienta inglesa *lah pee·meeyehn·tah een·gleh·sah* — allspice

el pimiento *ehl pee·meeyehn·toh* — pepper (vegetable)

la piña *lah pee·nyah* — pineapple

los piñones *lohs pee·nyohn·ehs* — pine nuts

la pintada *lah peen·tah·dah* — guinea fowl

la pizza *lah peeth·thah* — pizza

el plátano *ehl plah·tah·noh*	banana
el pollo *ehl poh·yoh*	chicken
el pollo frito *ehl poh·yoh free·toh*	fried chicken
el pomelo *ehl poh·meh·loh*	grapefruit
el puerro *ehl pweh·rroh*	leek
el pulpo *ehl pool·poh*	octopus
el queso *ehl keh·soh*	cheese
el queso de cabra *ehl keh·soh deh kah·brah*	goat cheese
el queso crema *ehl keh·soh kreh·mah*	cream cheese
el queso roquefort *ehl keh·soh roh·keh·fohrt*	blue cheese
el rábano *ehl rah·bah·noh*	radish
el rabo de buey *ehl rah·boh deh bwehy*	oxtail
el rape *ehl rah·peh*	monkfish
el ravioli *ehl rah·beeyoh·lee*	ravioli
la raya *lah rah·yah*	skate
el refresco *ehl reh·frehs·koh*	soda
relleno *reh·yeh·noh*	stuffed/stuffing
la remolacha *lah reh·moh·lah·chah*	beet
el repollo *ehl reh·poh·yoh*	cabbage
el requesón *ehl reh·keh·sohn*	cottage cheese
el requesón de soja *ehl reh·keh·sohn deh soh·khah*	tofu

los retoños de bambú *lohs reh•toh•nyohs deh bahm•boo* — bamboo shoots

el riñón *ehl ree•nyohn* — kidney

el róbalo *ehl roh•bah•loh* — haddock

el romero *ehl roh•meh•roh* — rosemary

el ron *ehl rohn* — rum

el rosbif *ehl rohs•beef* — roast beef

la rosquilla *lah rohs•kee•yah* — doughnut

rubia *roo•beeyah* — lager (beer)

el ruibarbo *ehl rwee•bahr•boh* — rhubarb

la sal *lah sahl* — salt

el salami *ehl sah•lah•mee* — salami

la salchicha *lah sahl•chee•chah* — sausage

el salmón *ehl sahl•mohn* — salmon

el salmonete *ehl sahl•moh•neh•teh* — red mullet

la salsa *lah sahl•sah* — sauce

la salsa agridulce *lah sahl•sah ah•gree•dool•theh* — sweet and sour sauce

la salsa alioli *lah sahl•sah ah•yee•oh•lee* — garlic sauce

la salsa picante *lah sahl•sah pee•kahn•teh* — hot pepper sauce

la salsa de soja *lah sahl•sah deh soh•khah* — soy sauce

la salvia *lah sahl•beeyah* — sage

la sandía *lah sahn•dee•ah* — watermelon

el sándwich *ehl sahnd•weech* — sandwich

la sangría *lah sahn•gree•ah* — wine punch

la sardina *lah sahr•dee•nah* — sardine

la semilla *lah seh•mee•yah* — seed

la semilla de soja *lah seh•mee•yah deh soh•khah* — soybean [soya bean]

el sésamo *ehl seh•sah•moh* — sesame

los sesos *lohs seh•sohs* — brains

la seta *lah <u>seh</u>·tah*	mushroom
la sidra *lah <u>see</u>·drah*	cider
el sifón *ehl see·<u>fohn</u>*	seltzer water
el sirope *ehl see·<u>roh</u>·peh*	syrup
la soja *lah <u>soh</u>·khah*	soy [soya]
el solomillo *ehl soh·loh·<u>mee</u>·yoh*	sirloin
la sopa *lah <u>soh</u>·pah*	soup
el sorbete *ehl sohr·<u>beh</u>·teh*	sorbet
el suero de leche *ehl <u>sweh</u>·roh deh <u>leh</u>·cheh*	buttermilk
la tarta *lah <u>tahr</u>·tah*	cake
el té *ehl teh*	tea
la ternera *lah tehr·<u>neh</u>·rah*	veal
el tequila *ehl teh·<u>kee</u>·lah*	tequila
el tiburón *ehl tee·boo·<u>rohn</u>*	shark
tinto *<u>teen</u>·toh*	red (wine)
el tocino *ehl toh·<u>thee</u>·noh*	bacon
el tofu *ehl <u>toh</u>·foo*	tofu
el tomate *ehl toh·<u>mah</u>·teh*	tomato
el tomillo *ehl toh·<u>mee</u>·yoh*	thyme
la tónica *lah <u>toh</u>·nee·kah*	tonic water
la tortilla *lah tohr·<u>tee</u>·yah*	omelet
la tortita *lah tohr·<u>tee</u>·tah*	large pancake served as an afternoon snack
la tostada *lah tohs·<u>tah</u>·dah*	toast
el trigo *ehl <u>tree</u>·goh*	wheat
la trucha *lah <u>troo</u>·chah*	trout
las trufas *lahs <u>troo</u>·fahs*	truffles
la uva *lah <u>oo</u>·bah*	grape
la vainilla *lah bayee·<u>nee</u>·yah*	vanilla
el venado *ehl beh·<u>nah</u>·doh*	venison
la verdura *lah behr·<u>doo</u>·rah*	vegetable

el vermut *ehl behr·moot*	vermouth
las vieiras *lahs bee·eyee·rahs*	scallop
el vinagre *ehl bee·nah·greh*	vinegar
el vino *ehl beeh·noh*	wine
el vino dulce *ehl bee·noh dool·theh*	dessert wine
el vodka *ehl bohd·kah*	vodka
el whisky *ehl wees·kee*	whisky
el whisky escocés *ehl wees·kee ehs·koh·thehs*	scotch
la yema/clara de huevo *lah yeh·mah/klah·rah deh weh·boh*	egg yolk/white
el yogur *ehl yoh·goor*	yogurt
la zanahoria *lah thah·nah·oh·reeyah*	carrot
la zarzamora *lah thahr·thah·moh·rah*	blackberry
el zumo *ehl thoo·moh*	juice

People

Conversation

ESSENTIAL

Hello!	**¡Hola!** _oh·lah_
How are you?	**¿Cómo está?** _koh·moh ehs·tah_
Fine, thanks.	**Bien, gracias.** _beeyehn grah·theeyahs_
Excuse me! (to get attention)	**¡Perdón!** _pehr·dohn_
Do you speak English?	**¿Habla inglés?** _ah·blah een·glehs_
What's your name?	**¿Cómo se llama?** _koh·moh seh yah·mah_
My name is…	**Me llamo…** _meh yah·moh…_
Nice to meet you.	**Encantado m/Encantada f.** _ehn·kahn·tah·doh/ehn·kahn·tah·dah_
Where are you from?	**¿De dónde es usted?** _deh dohn·deh ehs oos·teth_
I'm from the U.S./U.K.	**Soy de Estados Unidos/del Reino Unido.** _soy deh ehs·tah·dohs oo·nee·dohs/ dehl reyey·noh oo·nee·doh_
What do you do for a living?	**¿A qué se dedica?** _ah keh seh deh·dee·kah_
I work for…	**Trabajo para…** _trah·bah·khoh pah·rah…_
I'm a student.	**Soy estudiante.** _soy ehs·too·deeyahn·teh_
I'm retired.	**Estoy jubilado m/jubilada f.** _ehs·toy khoo·bee·lah·doh/khoo·bee·lah·dah_
Do you like…?	**¿Le gusta…?** _leh goos·tah…_
Goodbye.	**Adiós.** _ah·deeyohs_
See you later.	**Hasta luego.** _ah·stah lweh·goh_

For Grammar, see page 162.

When addressing strangers, always use the more formal **usted** (singular) or **ustedes** (plural), as opposed to the more familiar **tú** (singular) or **vosotros** (plural), until told otherwise. If you know someone's title, it's polite to use it, e.g., **doctor** (male doctor), **doctora** (female doctor). You can also simply say **Señor** (Mr.), **Señora** (Mrs.) or **Señorita** (Miss).

Language Difficulties

Do you speak English?	**¿Habla inglés?** _ah_·blah een·_glehs_
Does anyone here speak English?	**¿Hay alguien que hable inglés?** aye _ahl_·geeyenh keh _ah_·bleh een·_glehs_
I don't speak (much) Spanish.	**No hablo (mucho) español.** noh _ah_·bloh (_moo_·choh) ehs·pah·_nyol_
Can you speak more slowly?	**¿Puede hablar más despacio?** _pweh_·deh ah·_blahr_ mahs dehs·_pah_·theeyoh
Can you repeat that?	**¿Podría repetir eso?** poh·_dree_·ah reh·peh·_teer_ eh·soh
Excuse me?	**¿Cómo?** _koh_·moh
What was that?	**¿Qué ha dicho?** keh ah _dee_·choh
Can you spell it?	**¿Podría deletrearlo?** poh·_dree_·ah deh·leh·treh·_ahr_·loh
Please write it down.	**Escríbamelo, por favor.** ehs·_kree_·bah·meh·loh pohr fah·_bohr_

YOU MAY HEAR...

Hablo muy poco inglés.
_ah_·bloh mooy _poh_·koh een·_glehs_
No hablo inglés. noh _ah_·bloh een·_glehs_

I only speak a little English.
I don't speak English.

Can you translate this into English for me?	**¿Podría traducirme esto al inglés?** *poh·dree·ah trah·doo·theer·meh ehs·toh ahl een·glehs*
What does this/ that mean?	**¿Qué significa esto/eso?** *keh seeg·nee·fee·kah ehs·toh/eh·soh*
I understand.	**Entiendo.** *ehn·teeyehn·doh*
I don't understand.	**No entiendo.** *noh ehn·teeyehn·doh*
Do you understand?	**¿Entiende?** *ehn·teeyehn·deh*

Making Friends

Hello!	**¡Hola!** *oh·lah*
Good morning.	**Buenos días.** *bweh·nohs dee·ahs*
Good afternoon.	**Buenas tardes.** *bweh·nahs tahr·dehs*
Good evening.	**Buenas noches.** *bweh·nahs noh·chehs*
My name is...	**Me llamo...** *meh yah·moh...*
What's your name?	**¿Cómo se llama?** *koh·moh seh yah·mah*
I'd like to introduce you to...	**Quiero presentarle a...** *keeyeh·roh preh·sehn·tahr·leh ah...*
Pleased to meet you.	**Encantado *m*/Encantada *f*.** *ehn·kahn·tah·doh/ehn·kahn·tah·dah*
How are you?	**¿Cómo está?** *koh·moh ehs·tah*
Fine, thanks. And you?	**Bien gracias. ¿Y usted?** *beeyehn grah·theeyahs ee oos·tehth*

When first meeting someone in Spain always greet him or her with **hola** (hello), **buenos días** (good morning) or **buenas tardes** (good afternoon). Spaniards even extend this general greeting to strangers when in elevators, waiting rooms and other small public spaces. A general acknowledgment or reply is expected from all. When leaving, say **adiós** (goodbye).

Travel Talk

I'm here...	**Estoy aquí...**	*ehs·toy ah·kee...*
on business	**en viaje de negocios**	*ehn beeyah·kheh deh neh·goh·theeyohs*
on vacation	**de vacaciones**	*deh bah·kah·theeyoh·nehs*
studying	**estudiando**	*ehs·too·deeyahn·doh*
I'm staying for...	**Voy a quedarme...**	*boy ah keh·dahr·meh...*
I've been here...	**Llevo aquí...**	*yeh·boh ah·kee...*
a day	**un día**	*oon dee·ah*
a week	**una semana**	*oo·nah seh·mah·nah*
a month	**un mes**	*oon mehs*
Where are you from?	**¿De dónde es usted?**	*deh dohn·deh ehs oos·tehth*
I'm from...	**Soy de...**	*soy deh...*

For Numbers, see page 167.

Personal

Who are you with?	**¿Con quién ha venido?**	*kohn keeyehn ah beh·nee·doh*
I'm here alone.	**He venido solo** *m*/**sola** *f.*	*eh beh·nee·doh soh·loh/soh·lah*
I'm with my...	**He venido con mi...**	*eh beh·nee·doh kohn mee...*
husband/wife	**marido/mujer**	*mah·ree·doh/moo·khehr*
boyfriend/ girlfriend	**novio/novia**	*noh·beeyoh/ noh·beeyah*
friend	**amigo/amiga**	*ah·mee·goh/ah·mee·gah*
friends	**amigos/amigas**	*ah·mee·gohs/ah·mee·gahs*
colleague	**colega**	*koh·leh·gah*
colleagues	**colegas**	*koh·leh·gahs*
When's your birthday?	**¿Cuándo es su cumpleaños?**	*kwahn·doh ehs soo koom·pleh·ah·nyohs*
How old are you?	**¿Qué edad tiene usted?**	*keh eh·dahth teeyeh·neh oos·tehth*

I'm…	**Tengo…años.** *tehn•goh…ah•nyohs*
Are you married?	**¿Está casado m/casada f?** *ehs•tah kah•sah•doh/ kah•sah•dah*
I'm…	**Estoy…** *ehs•toy…*
single	**soltero m/soltera f** *sohl•teh•roh/sohl•teh•rah*
in a relationship	**en una relación** *ehn oo•nah reh•lah•theeyohn*
engaged	**comprometido m/comprometida f** *kohm•proh•meh•tee•doh/kohm•proh•meh•tee dah*
married	**casado m/casada f** *kah•sah•doh/kah•sah•dah*
divorced	**divorciado m/divorciada f** *dee•bohr•theeyah•doh/dee•bohr•theeyah•dah*
separated	**separado m/separada f** *seh•pah•rah•doh/ seh•pah•rah•dah*
I'm widowed.	**Soy viudo m/viuda f** *soy beeyoo•doh/beeyoo•dah*
Do you have children/ grandchildren?	**¿Tiene hijos/nietos?** *teeyeh•neh ee•khohs/neeyeh•tohs*

For Numbers, see page 167.

Work & School

What do you do for a living?	**¿A qué se dedica?** *ah keh seh deh•dee•kah*
What are you studying?	**¿Qué estudia?** *keh ehs•too•deeyah*
I'm studying Spanish.	**Estudio español.** *ehs•too•deeyoh ehs•pah•nyohl*
I…	**Yo…** *yoh…*
work full-time/ part-time	**trabajo a tiempo completo/parcial** *trah•bah•khoh ah teeyehm•poh kohm•pleh•toh/ pahr•theeyahl*
am unemployed	**estoy en el paro** *ehs•toy ehn ehl pah•roh*
work at home	**trabajo desde casa** *trah•bah•khoh dehs•deh kah•sah*

Who do you work for?	**¿Para quién trabaja?** _pah_•rah keeyehn trah•_bah_•khah
I work for…	**Trabajo para…** trah•_bah_•khoh _pah_•rah…
Here's my business card.	**Aquí tiene mi tarjeta.** ah•_kee_ _teeyeh_•neh mee tahr•_kheh_•tah

For Business Travel, see page 142.

Weather

What's the forecast?	**¿Cuál es el pronóstico del tiempo?** kwahl ehs ehl proh•_nohs_•tee•koh dehl _teeyehm_•poh
What beautiful/ terrible weather!	**¡Qué tiempo más bonito/feo hace!** keh _teeyehm_•poh mahs boh•_nee_•toh/_feh_•oh ah•theh
It's cool/warm.	**Está fresco/cálido** esh•_tah_ frehs•koh/_kah_•lee•doh
It's cold/hot.	**Hace frío/calor.** _ah_•theh _free_•oh/kah•_lohr_
It's rainy/sunny.	**Está lluvioso/soleado.** ehs•_tah_ yoo•_beeyoh_•soh/ soh•lee•_ah_•doh
It's snowy/icy.	**Hay nieve/hielo.** aye _neeyeh_•beh/_eeyeh_•loh
Do I need a jacket/an umbrella?	**¿Necesito una chaqueta/un paraguas?** neh•theh•_see_•toh _oo_•nah chah•_keh_•tah/oon pah•_rah_•gwahs

For Temperature, see page 174.

ESSENTIAL

Would you like to go out for a drink/dinner?	**¿Le gustaría salir a tomar una copa/cenar?** *leh goos·tah·ree·ah sah·leer ah toh·mahr oo·nah koh·pah/theh·nahr*
What are your plans for tonight/tomorrow?	**¿Qué planes tiene para esta noche/mañana?** *keh plah·nehs teeyeh·nehs pah·rah ehs·tah noh·cheh/mah·nyah·nah*
Can I have your number?	**¿Puede darme su número?** *pweh·deh dahr·meh soo noo·meh·roh*
Can I join you?	**¿Puedo acompañarle m/acompañarla f?** *pweh·doh ah·kohm·pah·nyahr·leh/ah·kohm·pah·nyahr·lah*
Can I buy you a drink?	**¿Puedo invitarle m/invitarla f a una copa?** *pweh·doh een·bee·tahr·leh/een·bee·tahr·lah ah oo·nah koh·pah*
I like you.	**Me gustas.** *meh goos·tahs*
I love you.	**Te quiero.** *teh keeyeh·roh*

The Dating Game

Would you like to go out for...?	**¿Le gustaría ir...?** *leh goos·tah·ree·ah eer...*
coffee	**a tomar un café** *ah toh·mahr oon kah·feh*
a drink	**a tomar un copa** *ah toh·mahr oo·nah koh·pah*
dinner	**a cenar** *ah theh·nahr*
What are your plans for...?	**¿Qué planes tiene para...?** *keh plahn·ehs teeyeh·neh pah·rah...*

today	**hoy** *oy*
tonight	**esta noche** *ehs·tah noh·cheh*
tomorrow	**mañana** *mah·nyah·nah*
this weekend	**este fin de semana** *ehs·teh feen deh seh·mah·nah*
Where would you like to go?	**¿Adónde le gustaría ir?** *ah dohn·deh leh goos·tah·ree·ah eer*
I'd like to go to...	**Me gustaría ir a...** *meh goos·tah·ree·ah eer ah...*
Do you like...?	**¿Le gusta...?** *leh goos·tah...*
Can I have your number/e-mail?	**¿Puede darme su número/dirección de correo electrónico?** *pweh·deh dahr·meh soo noo·meh·roh/dee·rehk·theeyohn deh koh·rreh·oh eh·lehk·troh·nee·koh*
Are you on Facebook/Twitter?	**¿Está en Facebook/Twitter?** *(polite form)* *ehs·tah ehn Facebook/Twitter*
	¿Estás en Facebook/Twitter? *(informal form)* *ehs·tahs ehn Facebook/Twitter*
Can I join you?	**¿Puedo acompañarle *m*/acompañarla *f*?** *pweh·doh ah·kohm·pah·nyahr·leh/ ah·kohm·pah·nyahr·lah*
You're very attractive.	**Eres muy guapo *m*/guapa *f*.** *eh·rehs mooy gwah·poh/gwah·pah*
Let's go somewhere quieter.	**Vayamos a un sitio más tranquilo.** *bah·yah·mohs ah oon see·teeyoh mahs trahn·kee·loh*

For Communications, see page 49.

Accepting & Rejecting

I'd love to.	**Me encantaría.** *meh ehn·kahn·tah·ree·yah*
Where should we meet?	**¿Dónde quedamos?** *dohn·deh keh·dah·mohs*
I'll meet you at the bar/your hotel.	**Quedamos en el bar/su hotel.** *keh·dah·mohs ehn ehl bahr/soo oh·tehl*

I'll come by at…	**Pasaré a recogerle m/recogerla f a las…**
	pah·sah·reh ah reh·koh·khehr·leh/
	reh·koh·khehr·lah ah lahs…
What is your address?	**¿Cuál es su dirección?** *kwahl ehs soo dee·rehk·theeyohn*
I'm busy.	**Estoy ocupado m/ocupada f.**
	ehs·toy oh·koo·pah·doh/oh·koo·pah·dah
I'm not interested.	**No me interesa.** *noh meh een·teh·reh·sah*
Leave me alone.	**Déjeme en paz.** *deh·kheh·meh ehn pahth*
Stop bothering me!	**¡Deje de molestarme!** *deh·kheh deh*
	moh·lehs·tahr·meh

For Time, see page 170.

Getting Intimate

Can I hug/kiss you?	**¿Puedo abrazarte/besarte?** *pweh·doh*
	ah·brah·thahr·teh/beh·sahr·teh
Yes.	**Sí.** *see*
No.	**No.** *noh*
Stop!	**¡Para!** *pah·rah*
I love you.	**Te quiero.** *teh keeyeh·roh*

Sexual Preferences

Are you gay?	**¿Eres gay?** *eh·rehs gay*
I'm…	**Soy…** *soy…*
heterosexual	**heterosexual** *eh·teh·roh·sehks·wahl*
homosexual	**homosexual** *oh·moh·sehks·wahl*
bisexual	**bisexual** *bee·sehks·wahl*
Do you like men/women?	**¿Te gustan los hombres/las mujeres?**
	teh goos·tahn lohs ohm·brehs/lahs moo·kheh·rehs

Leisure Time

Sightseeing

ESSENTIAL

Where's the tourist information office?	**¿Dónde está la oficina de turismo?** *dohn·deh ehs·tah lah oh·fee·thee·nah deh too·rees·moh*
What are the main sights?	**¿Dónde están los principales sitios de interés?** *dohn·deh ehs·tahn lohs preen·thee·pah·lehs see·teeyohs deh een·teh·rehs*
Do you have tours in English?	**¿Hay visitas en inglés?** *aye bee·see·tahs ehn een·glehs*
Can I have a map/guide?	**¿Puede darme un mapa/una guía?** *pweh·deh dahr·meh oon mah·pah/oo·nah gee·ah*

Tourist Information

Do you have information on…?	**¿Tiene información sobre…?** *teeyeh·neh een·fohr·mah·theeyohn soh·breh…*
Can you recommend…?	**¿Puede recomendarme…?** *pweh·deh reh·koh·mehn·dahr·meh…*
a bus tour	**un recorrido en autobús** *oon reh·koh·rree·doh ehn awtoh·boos*
an excursion to…	**una excursión a…** *oo·nah ehx·koor·seeyohn ah…*
a sightseeing tour	**un recorrido turístico** *oon reh·koh·rree·doh too·rees·tee·koh*

Tourist offices are located in major Spanish cities and in many of the smaller towns that are popular tourist attractions. Ask at your hotel or check online to find the nearest office.

On Tour

I'd like to go on the tour to…	**Quiero ir a la visita de…** _keeyeh•roh eer ah lah bee•see•tah deh…_
When's the next tour?	**¿Cuándo es la próxima visita?** _kwahn•doh ehs lah proh•xee•mah bee•see•tah_
Are there tours in English?	**¿Hay visitas en inglés?** _aye bee•see•tahs ehn een•glehs_
Is there an English guide book/audio guide?	**¿Hay una guía/audioguía en inglés?** _aye oo•nah gee•ah/awoo•deeyoh•gee•ah ehn een•glehs_
What time do we leave/return?	**¿A qué hora salimos/volvemos?** _ah keh oh•rah sah•lee•mohs/bohl•beh•mohs_
We'd like to see…	**Queremos ver…** _keh•reh•mohs behr…_
Can we stop here…?	**¿Podemos parar aquí…?** _poh•deh•mohs pah•rahr ah•kee…_
to take photos	**para tomar fotos** _pah•rah toh•mahr foh•tohs_
for souvenirs	**para comprar recuerdos** _pah•rah kohm•prahr reh•kwehr•dohs_
for the toilet	**para ir al servicio** _pah•rah eer ahl sehr•bee•theeyoh_
Is it disabled-accessible?	**¿Tiene acceso para discapacitados?** _teeyeh•neh ahk•theh•soh pah•rah dees•kah•pah•thee•tah•dohs_

Seeing the Sights

Where is/are…?	**¿Dónde está/están…?** _dohn•deh ehs•tah/ehs•tahn…_
the battleground	**el campo de batalla** _ehl kahm•poh deh bah•tah•yah_
the botanical garden	**el jardín botánico** _ehl khahr•deen boh•tah•nee•koh_
the castle	**el castillo** _ehl kahs•tee•yoh_
the downtown area	**el centro** _ehl thehn•troh_
the fountain	**la fuente** _lah fwehn•teh_
the library	**la biblioteca** _lah bee•bleeyoh•teh•kah_
the market	**el mercado** _ehl mehr•kah•doh_
the museum	**el museo** _ehl moo•seh•oh_

the old town	**el casco antiguo**	*ehl kahs•koh ahn•tee•gwoh*
the opera house	**teatro de la ópera**	*ehl tehahtroh deh lah operh rah*
the palace	**el palacio**	*ehl pah•lah•theeyoh*
the park	**el parque**	*ehl pahr•keh*
the ruins	**las ruinas**	*lahs rwee•nahs*
the shopping area	**la zona comercial**	*lahs thoh•nah koh•mehr•theeyahl*
the town square	**la plaza**	*lah plah•thah*
Can you show me on the map?	**¿Puede indicármelo en el mapa?**	*pweh•deh een•dee•kahr•meh•loh ehn ehl mah•pah*
It's...	**Es...**	*ehs...*
amazing	**increíble**	*een•kreh•ee•bleh*
beautiful	**precioso**	*preh•theeyoh•soh*
boring	**aburrido**	*ah•boo•rree•don*
interesting	**interesante**	*een•teh•reh•sahn•teh*
magnificent	**magnífico**	*mahg•nee•fee•koh*
romantic	**romántico**	*roh•mahn•tee•koh*
strange	**extraño**	*ex•trah•nyon*
stunning	**impresionante**	*eem•preh•seeyoh•nahn•teh*
terrible	**horrible**	*oh•rree•bleh*
ugly	**feo**	*feh•oh*
I (don't) like it.	**(No) Me gusta.**	*(noh) meh goo•stah*

Religious Sites

Where is…?	**¿Dónde está…?** <u>dohn</u>·deh ehs·<u>tah</u>…
the cathedral	**la catedral** lah kah·teh·<u>drahl</u>
the Catholic/	**la iglesia católica/protestante**
Protestant church	lah ee·<u>gleh</u>·seeyah kah·<u>toh</u>·lee·kah/proh·tehs·<u>tahn</u>·teh
the mosque	**la mezquita** lah mehth·<u>kee</u>·tah
the shrine	**el santuario** ehl sahn·<u>twah</u>·reeyoh
the synagogue	**la sinagoga** lah see·nah·<u>goh</u>·gah
the temple	**el templo** ehl <u>tehm</u>·ploh
What time is	**¿A qué hora es la misa/el culto?** ah keh
mass/the service?	<u>oh</u>·rah ehs lah <u>mee</u>·sah/ehl <u>kool</u>·toh

Shopping

ESSENTIAL

Where's the market/	**¿Dónde está el mercado/centro comercial?**
mall?	<u>dohn</u>·deh ehs·<u>tah</u> ehl mehr·<u>kah</u>·doh/
	<u>then</u>·troh koh·mehr·<u>theeyahl</u>
I'm just looking.	**Sólo estoy mirando.** <u>soh</u>·loh ehs·<u>toy</u> mee·<u>rahn</u>·doh
Can you help me?	**¿Puede ayudarme?** <u>pweh</u>·deh ah·yoo·<u>dahr</u>·meh
I'm being helped.	**Ya me atienden.** yah meh ah·<u>teeyehn</u>·dehn
How much?	**¿Cuánto es?** <u>kwahn</u>·toh ehs
That one, please.	**Ése m/Ésa f, por favor.** <u>eh</u>·she/<u>eh</u>·sah pohr fah·<u>bohr</u>
That's all.	**Eso es todo.** <u>eh</u>·soh ehs <u>toh</u>·doh
Where can I pay?	**¿Dónde se paga?** <u>dohn</u>·deh seh <u>pah</u>·gah
I'll pay in cash/by	**Voy a pagar en efectivo/con tarjeta de**
credit card.	**crédito.** boy ah pah·<u>gahr</u> ehn eh·fehk·<u>tee</u>·boh/
	kohn tahr·<u>kheh</u>·tah deh <u>kreh</u>·dee·toh
A receipt, please.	**Un recibo, por favor.** oon reh·<u>thee</u>·boh pohr fah·<u>bohr</u>

There are many types of markets in the towns of Spain. You can find a wide variety of goods at these markets, including fruit and vegetables, antiques, souvenirs, regional specialty items and so on. Your hotel or local tourist office will have information on the markets for your area. Most permanent markets are open daily from early morning till early afternoon; traveling market times vary by location. Inclement weather may cause a market to close early or not open at all.

At the Shops

Where is/are…?	**¿Dónde está/están…?**	_dohn•deh ehs•tah/ ehs•tahn_…
the antiques store	**la tienda de antigüedades**	_lah teeyehn•dah deh ahn•tee•gweh•dah•dehs_
the bakery	**la panadería**	_lah pah•nah•deh•ree•ah_
the bank	**el banco**	_ehl bahn•koh_
the bookstore	**la librería**	_lah lee•breh•ree•ah_
the clothing store	**la tienda de ropa**	_lah teeyehn•dah deh roh•pah_
the delicatessen	**la charcutería**	_lah chahr•koo•teh•ree•ah_
the department stores	**los grandes almacenes**	_lohs grahn•dehs ahl•mah•theh•nehs_
the gift shop	**la tienda de regalos**	_lah teeyehn•dah deh reh•gah•lohs_
the health food store	**la tienda de alimentos naturales**	_lah teeyehn•dah deh ah•lee•mehn•tohs nah•too•rahl•ehs_
the jeweler	**la joyería**	_lah khoh•yeh•ree•ah_
the liquor store [off-licence]	**la tienda de bebidas alcohólicas**	_lah teeyehn•dah deh beh•bee•dahs ahl•koh•oh•lee•kahs_
the market	**el mercado**	_ehl mehr•kah•doh_
the music store	**la tienda de música**	_lah teeyehn•dah deh moosee•kah_
the pastry shop	**la pastelería**	_lah pahs•teh•leh•ree•ah_

the pharmacy [chemist]	**la farmacia** *lah fahr•mah•theeyah*
the produce [grocery] store	**la tienda de frutas y verduras** *lah teeyehn•dah deh froo•tahs ee behr•doo•rahs*
the shoe store	**la zapatería** *lah thah•pah•teh•ree•ah*
the shopping mall	**el centro comercial** *ehl then•troh koh•mehr•theeyahl*
the souvenir store	**la tienda de recuerdos** *lah teeyehn•dah deh reh•kwehr•dohs*
the supermarket	**el supermercado** *ehl soo•pehr•mehr•kah•doh*
the tobacconist	**el estanco** *ehl ehs•tahn•koh*
the toy store	**la juguetería** *lah khoo•geh•teh•ree•ah*

Ask an Assistant

When do you open/close?	**¿A qué hora abren/cierran?** *ah keh oh•rah ah•brehn/theeyeh•rrahn*
Where is/are…?	**¿Dónde está/están…?** *dohn•deh ehs•tah/ehs•tahn…*
the cashier	**la caja** *lah kah•khah*
the escalators	**las escaleras mecánicas** *lahs ehs•kah•leh•rahs meh•kah•nee•kahs*
the elevator [lift]	**el ascensor** *ehl ahs•thehn•sohr*
the fitting room	**el probador** *ehl proh•bah•dohr*
the store directory	**la guía de tiendas** *lah gee•ah deh teeyehn•dahs*

YOU MAY SEE...

ABIERTO/CERRADO	open/closed
CERRADO AL MEDIODIA	closed for lunch
PROBADOR	fitting room
CAJERO m CAJERA f	cashier
SOLO EFECTIVO	cash only
SE ACEPTAN TARJETAS DE CREDITO	credit cards accepted
HORARIO DE APERTURA	business hours
SALIDA	exit

Can you help me?	**¿Puede ayudarme?** _pweh_·deh ah·yoo·_dahr_·meh
I'm just looking.	**Sólo estoy mirando.** _soh_·loh ehs·_toy_ mee·_rahn_·doh
I'm being helped.	**Ya me atienden.** yah meh ah·_teeyehn_·dehn
Do you have...?	**¿Tienen...?** _teeyeh_·nehn...
Can you show me...?	**¿Podría enseñarme...?** poh·_dree_·ah ehn·seh·_nyahr_·meh...
Can you ship/wrap it?	**¿Pueden hacer un envío/envolverlo?** _pweh_·dehn ah·_thehr_ oon ehn·_bee_·oh/ehn·bohl·_behr_·loh
How much?	**¿Cuánto es?** _kwahn_·toh ehs
That's all.	**Eso es todo.** _eh_·soh ehs _toh_·doh

For Clothing, see page 124.

YOU MAY HEAR...

¿Necesita ayuda? neh·theh·_see_·tah ah·_yoo_·dah	Can I help you?
Un momento. oon moh·_mehn_·toh	One moment.
¿Qué desea? keh deh·_seh_·ah	What would you like?
¿Algo más? _ahl_·goh mahs	Anything else?

Personal Preferences

I'd like something…	**Quiero algo…** _keeyeh•roh ahl•goh…_	
cheap/expensive	**barato/caro** _bah•rah•toh/kah•roh_	
larger/smaller	**más grande/más pequeño** _mahs grahn•deh/ mahs peh•keh•nyoh_	
from this region	**de esta región** _deh ehs•tah reh•kheeyohn_	
Around…euros.	**Alrededor de los…euros.** _ahl•reh•deh•dohr deh lohs… ew•rohs_	
Is it real?	**¿Es auténtico m/auténtica f?** _ehs awoo•tehn•tee•koh/awoo•tehn•tee•kah_	
Can you show me this/that?	**¿Puede enseñarme esto/eso?** _pweh•deh ehn•seh•nyahr•meh ehs•toh/eh•soh_	
That's not quite what I want.	**Eso no es realmente lo que busco.** _eh•soh noh ehs reh•ahl•mehn•teh loh keh boos•koh_	
No, I don't like it.	**No, no me gusta.** _noh noh meh goos•tah_	
It's too expensive.	**Es demasiado caro.** _ehs deh•mah•seeyah•doh kah•roh_	
I have to think about it.	**Quiero pensármelo.** _keeyeh•roh pehn•sahr•meh•loh_	
I'll take it.	**Me lo llevo.** _meh loh yeh•boh_	

Credit cards are widely accepted throughout Spain; you will need to show ID when using a credit card. Mastercard™ and Visa™ are the most commonly used; American Express® is accepted in most places. Debit cards are common in Spain and throughout Europe; these are usually accepted if backed by Visa™ or Mastercard™. Traveler's checks are not accepted everywhere; always have an alternate form of payment available. Cash is always accepted—some places, such as newsstands, tobacconists, flower shops and market or street stands, take cash only.

YOU MAY HEAR…

¿Cómo va a pagar? _koh•moh bah ah pah•gahr_   How are you paying?

Su tarjeta ha sido rechazada. _soo_   Your credit card has
tahr•kheh•tah ah see•doh reh•chah•thah•dah   been declined.

Su documento de identidad, por favor.   ID, please.
soo doh•koo•mehn•toh deh ee•dehn•tee•dahd
pohr fah•bohr

No aceptamos tarjetas de crédito.   We don't accept
noh ah•thehp•tah•mohs tahr•kheh•tahs deh   credit cards.
kreh•dee•toh

Sólo en efectivo, por favor. _soh•loh_   Cash only, please.
ehn eh•fehk•tee•boh pohr fah•bohr

¿Tiene cambio/billetes más pequeños?   Do you have change/
teeyeh•neh kahm•beeyoh/bee•yeh•tehs   small bills [notes]?
mahs peh•keh•nyohs

Paying & Bargaining

How much?	**¿Cuánto es?** _kwahn•toh ehs_
I'll pay…	**Voy a pagar…** _boy ah pah•gahr…_
in cash	**en efectivo** _ehn eh•fehk•tee•boh_
by credit card	**con tarjeta de crédito** _kohn tahr•kheh•tah_ _deh kreh•dee•toh_
by traveler's check [cheque]	**con cheque de viaje** _kohn cheh•keh deh_ _beeyah•kheh_
A receipt, please.	**Un recibo, por favor.** _oon reh•thee•boh pohr fah•bohr_
That's too much.	**Eso es demasiado.** _eh•soh ehs deh•mah•seeyah•doh_
I'll give you…	**Le doy…** _leh doy…_
I have only… euros.	**Sólo tengo…euros.** _soh•loh tehn•goh…ew•rohs_

Is that your best price?	**¿Es el mejor precio que me puede hacer?** *ehs ehl meh-khohr preh-theeyoh keh meh pweh-deh ah-thehr*
Can you give me a discount?	**¿Puede hacerme un descuento?** *pweh-deh ah-thehr-meh oon dehs-kwehn-toh*

For Numbers, see page 167.

Making a Complaint

I'd like…	**Quiero…** *keeyeh-roh…*
to exchange this	**cambiar esto por otro** *kahm-beeyahr ehs-toh pohr oh-troh*
to return this	**devolver esto** *deh-bohl-behr ehs-toh*
a refund	**que me devuelvan el dinero** *keh meh deh-bwehl-bahn ehl dee-neh-roh*
to see the manager	**hablar con el encargado** *ah-blahr kohn ehl ehn-kahr-gah-doh*

Services

Can you recommend…?	**¿Puede recomendarme…?** *pweh-deh reh-koh-mehn-dahr-meh*
a barber	**una peluquería de caballeros** *oo-nah peh-loo-keh-ree-ah deh kah-bah-yeh-rohs*
a dry cleaner	**una tintorería** *oo-nah teen-toh-reh-ree-ah*
a hairstylist	**una peluquería de señoras** *oo-nah peh-loo-keh-ree-ah deh seh-nyoh-rahs*
a laundromat [launderette]	**una lavandería** *oo-nah lah-bahn-deh-ree-ah*
a nail salon	**un salón de manicura** *sah-lohn deh mah-nee-koo-rah*
a spa	**un centro de salud y belleza** *oon then-troh deh sah-lood ee beh-yeh-thah*
a travel agency	**una agencia de viajes** *oo-nah ah-khehn-theeyah deh beeyah-khehs*

Can you...this?	**¿Puede...esto?** _pweh·deh...ehs·toh_
alter	**hacerle un arreglo a** _ah·thehr·leh oon ah·rreh·gloh ah_
clean	**limpiar** _leem·peeyahr_
fix	**zurcir** _thoor·theer_
press	**planchar** _plahn·chahr_
When will it be ready?	**¿Cuándo estará listo?** _kwahn·doh ehs·tah·rah lees·toh_

Hair & Beauty

I'd like...	**Quiero...** _keeyeh·roh..._
an appointment for today/tomorrow	**pedir hora para hoy/mañana** _peh·deer oh·rah pah·rah oy/mah·nyah·nah_
some color	**teñirme el pelo** _teh·nyeer·meh ehl peh·loh_
some highlights	**hacerme mechas** _ah·thehr·meh meh·chahs_
my hair styled/ blow-dried	**hacerme un peinado** _ah·thehr·meh oon peyee·nah·doh_
a haircut	**cortarme el pelo** _kohr·tahr·meh ehl peh·loh_

With its varied landscapes and more than 2,000 registered springs (mineral and other), Spain is a prime location for spas, wellness centers and health-based resorts. These facilities offer a variety of treatments, including relaxation therapies and herbal remedies. Day spas can be found throughout the country, especially in the larger cities, and resort and overnight spas often offer individual services to those not staying there. Many of these also offer a wide variety of other relaxing activities such as horseback riding, guided tours, golf and swimming. Some spas and resorts do not allow children, so check before booking if you are traveling with kids.

an eyebrow/	**depilarme las cejas/ingles**
bikini wax	*deh·pee·lahr·meh lahs theh·khahs/een·glehs*
a facial	**hacerme una limpieza de cutis**
	ah·thehr·meh oo·nah leem·peeyeh·thah deh koo·tees
a manicure/	**hacerme la manicura/pedicura**
pedicure	*ah·thehr·meh lah mah·nee·koo·rah/peh·dee·koo·rah*
a (sports) massage	**un masaje (deportivo)** *oon mah·sah·kheh*
	(deh·pohr·tee·boh)
a trim	**cortarme las puntas** *kohr·tahr·meh lahs poon·tahs*
Not too short.	**No me lo corte demasiado.** *noh meh loh kohr·teh*
	deh·mah·seeyah·doh
Shorter here.	**Quíteme más de aquí.** *kee·teh·meh mahs deh ah·kee*
Do you offer…?	**¿Hacen…?** *ah·thehn…*
acupuncture	**acupuntura** *ah·koo·poon·too·rah*
aromatherapy	**aromaterapia** *ah·roh·mah·teh·rah·peeyah*
oxygen treatment	**oxígenoterapia** *oh·xee·kheh·noh·teh·rah·peeyah*
Do you have	**¿Tienen una sauna?** *teeyehn·ehn oo·nah*
a sauna?	*sawoo·nah*

Antiques

How old is it?	**¿Qué antigüedad tiene?** *keh ahn·tee·gweh·dahd*
	teeyeh·neh
Do you have anything	**¿Tiene algo de la época…?** *teeyeh·neh*
from the…period?	*ahl·goh deh lah eh·poh·kah…*
Do I have to fill out	**¿Tengo que rellenar algún impreso?**
any forms?	*tehn·goh keh reh·yeh·nahr ahl·goon eem·preh·soh*
Is there a certificate	**¿Tiene el certificado de autenticidad?**
of authenticity?	*teeyeh·neh ehl thehr·tee·fee·kah·doh*
	deh awoo·tehn·tee·thee·dahd
Can you ship/wrap it?	**¿Puede llevármelo/envolvérmelo?**
	pweh·deh yeh·bahr·meh·loh/ehn·bohl·behr·meh·loh

YOU MAY HEAR...

Le queda genial *leh keh·dah kheh·neeyahl*
That looks great on you.
¿Cómo le queda? *koh·moh meh khe·dah*
How does it fit?
No tenemos su talla
noh teh·neh·mohs soo tah·yah
We don't have your size.

Clothing

I'd like...	**Quiero...** *keeyeh·roh...*
Can I try this on?	**¿Puedo probarme esto?** *pweh·doh proh·bahr·meh ehs·toh*
It doesn't fit.	**No me queda bien.** *noh meh keh·dah beeyehn*
It's too...	**Me queda demasiado...** *meh keh·dah deh·mah·seeyah·doh...*
big/small	**grande/pequeño m/pequeña f** *grahn·deh/peh·keh·nyoh/peh·keh·nyah*
short/long	**corto m/corta f/largo m/larga f** *kohr·toh/kohr·tah/lahr·goh/lahr·gah*
tight/loose	**ajustado/ancho** *ah·khoos·tah·doh/ahn·choh*
Do you have this in size...?	**¿Tiene esto en la talla...?** *teeyeh·neh ehs·toh ehn lah tah·yah...*
Do you have this in a bigger/smaller size?	**¿Tiene esto en una talla más grande/pequeña?** *teeyeh·neh ehs·toh ehn oo·nah tah·yah mahs grahn·deh/peh·keh·nyah*

YOU MAY SEE...

ROPA DE CABALLERO	men's clothing
ROPA DE SEÑORA	women's clothing
ROPA DE NIÑOS	children's clothing

Colors

I'd like something...	**Busco algo...** _boos_·koh _ahl_·goh...
beige	**beis** behyees
black	**negro** _neh_·groh
blue	**azul** ah·_thool_
brown	**marrón** mah·_rrohn_
green	**verde** _behr_·deh
gray	**gris** grees
orange	**naranja** nah·_rahn_·khah
pink	**rosa** _roh_·sah
purple	**morado** moh·_rah_·doh
red	**rojo** _roh_·khoh
white	**blanco** _blahn_·koh
yellow	**amarillo** ah·mah·_ree_·yoh

Clothes & Accessories

a backpack	**la mochila** lah moh·_chee_·lah
a belt	**el cinturón** ehl theen·too·_rohn_
a bikini	**el bikini** ehl bee·_kee_·nee
a blouse	**la blusa** lah _bloo_·sah
a bra	**el sujetador** ehl soo·kheh·tah·_dohr_
briefs/panties	**los calzoncillos/las bragas** lohs kahl·thohn·_thee_·yohs/lahs brah·gahs
a coat	**el abrigo** ehl ah·_bree_·goh
a dress	**el vestido** ehl behs·_tee_·doh
a hat	**el sombrero** ehl sohm·_breh_·roh
a jacket	**la chaqueta** lah chah·_keh_·tah
jeans	**los vaqueros** lohs bah·_keh_·rohs
pajamas	**el pijama** ehl pee·_khah_·mah
pants [trousers]	**los pantalones** lohs pahn·tah·_loh_·nehs
pantyhose [tights]	**las medias** lahs _meh_·deeyahs
a purse [handbag]	**el bolso** ehl _bohl_·soh

a raincoat	**el impermeable** *ehl eem·pehr·meh·<u>ah</u>·bleh*
a scarf	**la bufanda** *lah boo·<u>fahn</u>·dah*
a shirt	**la camisa** *lah kah·<u>mee</u>·sah*
shorts	**los pantalones cortos** *lohs pahn·tah·<u>loh</u>·nehs <u>kohr</u>·tohs*
a skirt	**la falda** *lah <u>fahl</u>·dah*
socks	**los calcetines** *lohs kahl·theh·<u>tee</u>·nehs*
a suit	**el traje de chaqueta** *ehl <u>trah</u>·kheh deh chah·<u>keh</u>·tah*
sunglasses	**las gafas de sol** *lahs <u>gah</u>·fahs deh sohl*
a sweater	**el jersey** *ehl khehr·<u>seyee</u>*
a sweatshirt	**la sudadera** *lah soo·dah·<u>deh</u>·rah*
a swimsuit	**el bañador** *ehl bah·nyah·<u>dohr</u>*
a T-shirt	**la camiseta** *lah kah·mee·<u>seh</u>·tah*
a tie	**la corbata** *lah kohr·<u>bah</u>·tah*
underwear	**la ropa interior** *lah <u>roh</u>·pah een·teh·<u>reeyohr</u>*

Fabric

I'd like...	**Quiero...** *<u>keeyeh</u>·roh...*
cotton	**algodón** *ahl·goh·<u>dohn</u>*
denim	**tela vaquera** *<u>teh</u>·lah bah·<u>keh</u>·rah*
lace	**encaje** *ehn·<u>kah</u>·kheh*
leather	**cuero** *<u>kweh</u>·roh*
linen	**lino** *<u>lee</u>·noh*
silk	**seda** *<u>seh</u>·dah*
wool	**lana** *<u>lah</u>·nah*
Is it machine washable?	**¿Se puede lavar a máquina?** *seh <u>pweh</u>·deh lah·<u>bahr</u> ah <u>mah</u>·kee·nah*

Shoes

I'd like...	**Quiero...** *<u>keeyeh</u>·roh...*
high-heels/flats	**zapatos de tacón/planos** *thah·<u>pah</u>·tohs deh tah·<u>kohn</u>/<u>plah</u>·nohs*
boots	**botas** *<u>boh</u>·tahs*

loafers	**mocasines** moh·kah·_see_·nehs
sandals	**sandalias** sahn·_dah_·leeyahs
shoes	**zapatos** thah·_pah_·tohs
slippers	**zapatillas** thah·pah·_tee_·yahs
sneakers	**zapatillas de deporte** thah·pah·_tee_·yahs deh deh·_pohr_·teh

In size... **En la talla...** ehn lah _tah_·yah...

For Numbers, see page 167.

Sizes

small (S)	**pequeña (P)** peh·_keh_·nyah (peh)
medium (M)	**mediana (M)** meh·_deeyah_·nah (ehm)
large (L)	**grande (G)** _grahn_·deh (kheh)
extra large (XL)	**XL** ehkees·ehleh
petite	**tallas pequeñas** _tah_·yahs peh·_keh_·nyahs
plus size	**tallas grandes** _tah_·yahs _grahn_·dehs

Newsagent & Tobacconist

Do you sell English-language newspapers?	**¿Venden periódicos en inglés?** _behn_·dehn peh·_reeyoh_·dee·kohs ehn een·_glehs_
I'd like...	**Quiero...** _keeyeh_·roh...
candy [sweets]	**caramelos** kah·rah·_meh_·lohs
chewing gum	**chicle** _chee_·kleh
a chocolate bar	**una chocolatina** _oo_·nah choh·koh·lah·_tee_·nah
a cigar	**un puro** oon _poo_·roh
a pack/carton of cigarettes	**un paquete/cartón de tabaco** oon pah·_keh_·teh/kahr·_tohn_ deh tah·_bah_·koh
a lighter	**un mechero** oon meh·_cheh_·roh
a magazine	**una revista** _oo_·nah reh·_bees_·tah
matches	**cerillas** theh·_ree_·yahs
a newspaper	**un periódico** oon peh·_reeyoh_·dee·koh
a pen	**un bolígrafo** oon boh·_lee_·grah·foh

a postcard	**una postal** _oo_•nah pohs•_tahl_
a road/town map of...	**un mapa de las carreteras/plano de...** oon _mah_•pah deh lahs kah•rreh•_teh_•rahs/_plah_•noh deh...
stamps	**sellos** _seh_•yohs

Photography

I'd like a/an... camera.	**Quiero una cámara...** _keeyeh_•roh _oo_•nah _kah_•mah•rah...
automatic	**automática** awoo•toh•_mah_•tee•kah
digital	**digital** dee•khee•_tahl_
disposable	**desechable** deh•seh•_chah_•bleh
I'd like...	**Quiero...** _keeyeh_•roh...
a battery	**una pila** _oo_•nah _pee_•lah
digital prints	**fotos digitales** _foh_•tohs dee•khee•_tah_•lehs
a memory card	**una tarjeta de memoria** _oo_•nah tahr•_kheh_•tah deh meh•_moh_•reeyah
Can I print digital photos here?	**¿Puedo imprimir aquí fotos digitales?** _pweh_•doh eem•pree•_meer_ ah•_kee_ _foh_•tohs dee•khee•_tah_•lehs

Souvenirs

bottle of wine	**la botella de vino** lah boh•_teh_•yah deh _bee_•noh
box of chocolates	**la caja de bombones** lah _kah_•khah deh bohm•_boh_•nehs
castanets	**las castañuelas** lahs kahs•tah•_nyweh_•lahs
doll	**la muñeca** lah moo•_nyeh_•kah
fan (wooden, flamenco)	**el abanico de madera** ehl ah•bah•_nee_•koh deh mah•_deh_•rah
key ring	**el llavero** ehl yah•_beh_•roh
postcard	**la postal** lah pohs•_tahl_
pottery	**la cerámica** lah theh•_rah_•mee•kah
serrano ham	**el jamón serrano** ehl khah•_mohn_ seh•_rrah_•noh
T-shirt	**la camiseta** lah kah•mee•_seh_•tah
terracotta bowl	**la cazuela de barro** lah kah•_thweh_•lah deh _bah_•rroh

Spain produces a wide range of souvenirs, from typical tourist T-shirts to high-quality regional crafts. Spanish wine is popular and quality examples, such as sherry from Jerez and red wine from Rioja, can be found all over. Olive oil is also a popular gift. Classic Spanish souvenirs include bullfighting mementos, such as figurines, posters or capes, castanets, hand-painted flamenco fans and guitars. Reproduction paintings by Spain's most famous artists, such as Picasso, Dalí, Miró, Goya, El Greco or Velázquez, are also popular. Specialty regional goods include copperware, earthenware, leather goods, jewelry, lace, porcelain and wood carvings. Spanish swords and other metal work from Toledo are unique gifts, and Lladro® porcelain figurines are very popular. To find a good representation of each region's specialty goods at reasonable prices, visit the markets in each town.

toy	**el juguete** *ehl khoo·geh·teh*
wine	**el vino** *ehl bee·noh*
Can I see this/that?	**¿Puedo ver esto/eso?** *pweh·doh behr ehs·toh/eh·soh*
It's in the window/ display case.	**Está en el escaparate/la vitrina.** *ehs·tah ehn ehl ehs·kah·pah·rah·teh/lah bee·tree·nah*
I'd like…	**Quiero…** *keeyeh·roh…*
a battery	**una pila** *oo·nah pee·lah*
a bracelet	**una pulsera** *oo·nah pool·seh·rah*
a brooch	**un broche** *oon broh·cheh*
earrings	**unos pendientes** *oo·nohs pehn·deeyehn·tehs*
a necklace	**un collar** *oon koh·yahr*
a ring	**un anillo** *oon ah·nee·yoh*
a watch	**un reloj de pulsera** *oon reh·lohkh deh pool·seh·rah*
I'd like…	**Quiero…** *keeyeh·roh…*
copper	**cobre** *koh·breh*

crystal	**cristal** krees·_tahl_	
diamonds	**diamantes** deeyah·_mahn_·tehs	
white/yellow gold	**oro blanco/amarillo** _oh_·roh _blahn_·koh/ah·mah·_ree_·yoh	
pearls	**perlas** _pehr_·lahs	
pewter	**peltre** _pehl_·treh	
platinum	**platino** plah·_tee_·noh	
sterling silver	**plata esterlina** _plah_·tah ehs·tehr·_lee_·nah	
Is this real?	**¿Es auténtico?** ehs awoo·_tehn_·tee·koh	
Can you engrave it?	**¿Puede grabármelo?** _pweh_·deh grah·_bahr_·meh·loh	

Sport & Leisure

ESSENTIAL

When's the game?	**¿Cuándo empieza el partido?**
	kwahn·doh ehm·_peeyeh_·thah ehl pahr·_tee_·doh
Where's...?	**¿Dónde está...?** _dohn_·deh ehs·_tah_...
the beach	**la playa** lah _plah_·yah
the park	**el parque** ehl _pahr_·keh
the pool	**la piscina** lah pees·_thee_·nah
Is it safe to swim here?	**¿Es seguro nadar aquí?** ehs seh·_goo_·roh nah·_dahr_ ah·_kee_
Can I rent [hire] golf clubs?	**¿Puedo alquilar palos de golf?** _pweh_·doh ahl·kee·_lahr_ pah·lohs deh golf
How much per hour?	**¿Cuánto cuesta por hora?** _kwahn_·toh _kwehs_·tah pohr _oh_·rah
How far is it to...?	**¿A qué distancia está...?** ah keh dees·_tahn_·theeyah ehs·_tah_...
Can you show me on the map, please?	**¿Puede indicármelo en el mapa, por favor?** _pweh_·deh een·dee·_kahr_·meh·loh ehn ehl _mah_·pah pohr fah·_bohr_

Watching Sport

When's…?	**¿Cuándo empieza…?**
	kwahn·doh ehm·peeyeh·thah…
the baseball game	**el juego del béisbol** _ehl khooeh·goh dehl behees·bohl_
the basketball game	**el partido de baloncesto** _ehl pahr·tee·doh deh bah·lohn·thehs·toh_
the boxing match	**la pelea de boxeo** _lah peh·leh·ah deh bohks·eh·oh_
the cycling race	**la vuelta ciclista** _lah bwehl·tah thee·klees·tah_
the golf tournament	**el torneo de golf** _ehl tohr·neh·oh deh golf_
the soccer [football] game	**el partido de fútbol** _ehl pahr·tee·doh deh foot·bohl_
the tennis match	**el partido de tenis** _ehl pahr·tee·doh deh teh·nees_
the volleyball game	**el partido de voleibol** _ehl pahr·tee·doh deh boh·leyee·bohl_
Who's playing?	**¿Quienes juegan?** _keeyeh·nehs khweh·gahn_
Where is…?	**¿Dónde está…?** _dohn·deh ehs·tah…_
the horsetrack	**el hipódromo** _ehl ee·poh·droh·moh_
the racetrack	**el circuito de carreras** _ehl theer·kwee·toh de kah·rreh·rahs_
the stadium	**el estadio** _ehl ehs·tah·deeyoh_
Where can I place a bet?	**¿Dónde puedo hacer una apuesta?** _dohn·deh pweh·doh ah·thehr oo·nah ah·pwehs·tah_

Playing Sport

Where is/are…?	**¿Dónde está/están…?** _dohn·deh ehs·tah/ ehs·tahn…_
the golf course	**el campo de golf** _ehl kahm·poh deh golf_
the gym	**el gimnasio** _ehl kheem·nah·seeyoh_
the park	**el parque** _ehl pahr·keh_
the tennis courts	**las canchas de tenis** _lahs kahn·chahs deh teh·nees_

How much per...?	**¿Cuánto cuesta por...?** _kwahn_·toh _kwehs_·tah pohr...
day	**día** _dee_·ah
hour	**hora** _oh_·rah
game	**partido** pahr·_tee_·doh
round	**juego** _khweh_·goh
Can I rent [hire]...?	**¿Puedo alquilar...?** _pweh_·doh ahl·kee·_lahr_...
golf clubs	**palos de golf** _pah_·lohs deh golf
equipment	**equipo** eh·_kee_·poh
a racket	**una raqueta** _oo_·nah rah·_keh_·tah

At the Beach/Pool

Where's the beach/pool?	**¿Dónde está la playa/piscina?** _dohn_·deh ehs·_tah_ lah _plah_·yah/pees·_thee_·nah
Is there...?	**¿Hay...?** aye...
a kiddie pool	**una piscina infantil** _oo_·nah pees·_thee_·nah een·fahn·_teel_
an indoor/ outdoor pool	**una piscina cubierta/exterior** _oo_·nah pees·_thee_·nah koo·_beeyehr_·tah/ehx·teh·_reeyohr_
a lifeguard	**un socorrista** oon soh·koh·_rrees_·tah
Is it safe...?	**¿Es seguro...?** ehs seh·_goo_·roh...
to swim	**nadar** nah·_dahr_
to dive	**tirarse de cabeza** tee·_rahr_·seh deh kah·_beh_·thah

Fútbol (soccer) is the most popular sport in Spain; most cities in Spain have their own professional teams with a large fan base. Note that fans are extremely dedicated, so be sure not to insult the team. Almost all activity in Spain stops when there is an important soccer game on.

Golf is also popular and the golf courses on the Costa del Sol are worth a round. Other popular sports include basketball, tennis, auto racing, horse racing, hiking and climbing. **Jai alai** is a popular fast-paced game involving balls and curved -wicker-basket gloves.

There are many casinos throughout Spain. Minimum entrance and gaming age is 18; ID is required and the dress code is business casual.

for children	**para los niños** _pah_•rah lohs _nee_•nyohs
I'd like to hire…	**Quiero alquilar…** _keeyeh_•roh ahl•kee•_lahr_…
a deck chair	**una tumbona** _oo_•nah toom•_boh_•nah
diving equipment	**equipo de buceo** eh•_kee_•poh deh boo•_theh_•oh
a jet ski	**una moto acuática** _oo_•nah _moh_•toh ah•_kwah_•tee•kah
a motorboat	**una lancha motora** _oo_•nah _lahn_•chah moh•_toh_•rah
a rowboat	**una barca de remos** _oo_•nah _bahr_•kah deh _reh_•mohs
snorkeling equipment	**equipo de esnórquel** eh•_kee_•poh deh ehs•_nohr_•kehl
a surfboard	**una tabla de surf** _oo_•nah _tah_•blah deh soorf
a towel	**una toalla** _oo_•nah toh•_ah_•yah
an umbrella	**una sombrilla** _oo_•nah sohm•_bree_•yah
water skis	**unos esquís acuáticos** _oo_•nohs ehs•_kees_ ah•_kwah_•tee•kohs
a windsurfer	**una tabla de windsurf** _oo_•nah _tah_•blah deh _weend_•soorf
For…hours.	**Por…horas.** pohr… _oh_•rahs

Winter Sports

A lift pass for a day/five days, please.	**Un pase de un día/cinco días de acceso a los remontes.** oon pah·seh deh oon dee·ah/theen·koh dee·ahs deh ahk·theh·soh ah lohs reh·mohn·tehs
I'd like to hire [hire]...	**Quiero alquilar...** keeyeh·roh ahl·kee·lahr...
boots	**botas** boh·tahs
a helmet	**un casco** oon kahs·koh
poles	**bastones** bahs·toh·nehs
skis	**esquís** ehs·kees
a snowboard	**una tabla de snowboard** oo·nah tah·blah deh snoh·bohrd
snowshoes	**raquetas de nieve** rah·keh·tahs deh neeyeh·beh
Are there lessons?	**¿Dan clases?** dahn klah·sehs
These are too big/small.	**Me quedan demasiado grandes/pequeños.** meh keh·dahn deh·mah·seeyah·doh grahn·dehs/peh·keh·nyohs
I'm a beginner.	**Soy principiante.** soy preen·thee·peeyahn·teh
I'm experienced.	**Tengo experiencia.** tehn·goh ehx·peh·reeyehn·theeyah
A trail [piste] map, please.	**Un mapa de las pistas, por favor.** oon mah·pah deh lahs pees·tahs pohr fah·bohr

Out in the Country

A map of..., please.	**Un mapa de..., por favor.** oon mah·pah deh... pohr fah·bohr
this region	**esta región** ehs·tah reh·kheeyohn
the walking routes	**las rutas de senderismo** lahs roo·tahs deh sehn·deh·rees·moh
the bike routes	**los senderos para bicicletas** lohs sehn·deh·rohs pah·rah bee·thee·kleh·tahs
the trails	**los senderos** lohs sehn·deh·rohs
Is it... easy/difficult?	**¿Es... fácil/difícil?** ehs fah·theel/dee·fee·theel

Spain has more than 2,400 miles (4,000 km) of coastline and more than 1,700 beaches, with 16 different **Costas** (coastal regions). Two of the more famous coastal regions are **Costa del Sol** and **Costa Blanca**. Spain's Balearic and Canary Islands boast some of the most beautiful beaches in the world. If you decide to go for a swim, check the safety flags at each beach. Green flags indicate the water is safe, yellow flags indicate that you should use caution and red flags indicate that the water is unsafe for swimming.

Is it far/steep?	**¿Está lejos/empinado?** *ehs•tah leh•khohs/ ehm•pee•nah•doh*
I'm lost.	**Me he perdido.** *meh eh pehr•dee•doh*
How far is it to…?	**¿A qué distancia está…?** *ah keh dees•tahn•theeyah ehs•tah…*
Can you show me on the map, please?	**¿Puede indicármelo en el mapa, por favor?** *pweh•deh een•dee•kahr•meh•loh ehn ehl mah•pah pohr fah•bohr*
Where is…?	**¿Dónde está…?** *dohn•deh ehs•tah…*
the bridge	**el puente** *ehl pwehn•teh*

Spain has three mountain ranges, the Pyrenees, the Sierra Nevada and the Cantabrian, with an average altitude of 2,000 feet (600 m). There are more than 30 ski resorts throughout Spain with more than 620 miles (1,000 km) of ski runs combined. In addition to skiing, most resorts and ski areas offer other winter activities such as snowboarding, snowmobiling, sledding and dog-sledding.

the cave	**la cueva**	lah _kweh_•bah
the cliff	**el acantilado**	ehl ah•kahn•tee•_lah_•doh
the desert	**el desierto**	ehl deh•_seeyehr_•toh
the farm	**la granja**	lah _grahn_•khah
the field	**el campo**	ehl _kahm_•poh
the forest	**el bosque**	ehl _bohs_•keh
the hill	**la colina**	lah koh•_lee_•nah
the lake	**el lago**	ehl _lah_•goh
the mountain	**la montaña**	lah mohn•_tah_•nyah
the nature preserve	**la reserva natural**	lah reh•_sehr_•bah nah•too•_rahl_
the viewpoint	**el mirador**	ehl mee•rah•_dohr_
the park	**el parque**	ehl _pahr_•keh

YOU MAY SEE…

TELESQUÍ	drag lift
TELEFÉRICO	cable car
TELESILLA	chair lift
PRINCIPIANTE	novice
NIVEL INTERMEDIO	intermediate
EXPERTO	expert
PISTA CERRADA	trail [piste] closed

the path	**el camino** *ehl kah•mee•noh*
the peak	**el pico** *ehl pee•koh*
the picnic area	**la zona de picnic** *lah thoh•nah deh peek•neek*
the pond	**el estanque** *ehl ehs•tahn•keh*
the river	**el río** *ehl ree•oh*
the sea	**el mar** *ehl mahr*
the (thermal)	**el manantial (de aguas termales)**
spring	*ehl mah•nahn•teeyahl (deh ah•gwahs tehr•mah•lehs)*
the stream	**el arroyo** *ehl ah•rroh•yoh*
the valley	**el valle** *ehl bah•yeh*
the vineyard	**la viña** *lah bee•nyah*
the waterfall	**la cascada** *lah kahs•kah•dah*

Going Out

ESSENTIAL

What's there to do at night?	**¿Qué se puede hacer por las noches?** *keh seh pweh•deh ah•thehr pohr lahs noh•chehs*
Do you have a program of events?	**¿Tiene un programa de espectáculos?** *teeyeh•neh oon proh•grah•mah deh ehs•pehk•tah•koo•lohs*
What's playing tonight?	**¿Qué hay en cartelera esta noche?** *keh aye ehn kahr•teh•leh•rah ehs•tah noh•cheh*
Where's…?	**¿Dónde está…?** *dohn•deh ehs•tah…*
the downtown area	**el centro** *ehl thehn•troh*
the bar	**el bar** *ehl bahr*
the dance club	**la discoteca** *lah dees•koh•teh•kah*
Is there a cover charge?	**¿Hay que pagar entrada?** *aye keh pah•gahr ehn•trah•dah*

Spain is famous for its centuries-old tradition of bullfighting. Known as **tauromaquia** or **corrida de toros**, bullfighting is seen as an art and tradition by many, and as a cruel and violent act against animals by others. Whether you find it fascinating or appalling, the bullfight is a unique experience in Spain. The bullfighting season runs from March to October; many towns have a vibrant festival in March to open the season.

Entertainment

Can you recommend…?	**¿Puede recomendarme…?** _pweh·deh reh·koh·mehn·dahr·meh…_
a concert	**un concierto** _oon kohn·theeyehr·toh_
a movie	**una película** _oo·nah peh·lee·koo·lah_
an opera	**una ópera** _oo·nah oh·peh·rah_
a play	**una obra de teatro** _oo·nah oh·brah deh teh·ah·troh_
When does it start/end?	**¿A qué hora empieza/termina?** _ah keh oh·rah ehm·peeyeh·thah/tehr·mee·nah_
What's the dress code?	**¿Cómo hay que ir vestido m/vestida f?** _koh·moh aye keh eer behs·tee·doh/behs·tee·dah_
I like…	**Me gusta…** _meh goos·tah…_
classical music	**la música clásica** _lah moo·see·kah klah·see·kah_
folk music	**la música folk** _lah moo·see·kah folk_
jazz	**el jazz** _ehl jazz_
pop music	**la música pop** _lah moo·see·kah pop_
rap	**el rap** _ehl rap_

For Tickets, see page 19.

Nightlife

What's there to do at night?	**¿Qué se puede hacer por las noches?** *keh seh pweh·deh ah·thehr pohr lahs noh·chehs*
Can you recommend...?	**¿Puede recomendarme...?** *pweh·deh reh·koh·mehn·dahr·meh...*
a bar	**un bar** *oon bahr*
a cabaret	**un cabaré** *oon kah·bah·reh*
a casino	**un casino** *oon kah·see·noh*
a dance club	**una discoteca** *oo·nah dees·koh·teh·kah*
a flamenco performance	**un espectáculo de flamenco** *oon ehs·pehk·tah·koo·loh deh flah·mehn·koh*
a gay club	**una discoteca gay** *oo·nah dees·koh·teh·kah gay*

Tourist offices, travel agencies and guidebooks have extensive information regarding events throughout Spain. Dates of some annual events change each year, so check before you go. For listings of local events, check the daily newspapers or ask at your hotel or the local tourist office. Larger cities in Spain have many entertainment magazines and publications that are a good source for information. A few of the most popular annual events are listed below.

Carnaval is the festival that takes place the week before Lent. It's the Spanish equivalent of Mardi Gras.

Traditional Holy Week festivities are centered around Catholicism. Seville has some of the most spectacular and elaborate processional re-enactments of the religious events of Easter. Valencia is famous for building, then torching, giant papier-mâché figures.

The **Fiesta de San Fermín** is one of Spain's most famous events. The running of the bulls is an annual event that draws thousands of people to Pamplona and is televised worldwide.

YOU MAY HEAR...

Por favor apaguen sus teléfonos móviles.
*pohr fah·bohr ah·pah·gehn soos
teh·leh·foh·nohs moh·bee·lehs*

Turn off your cell [mobile] phones, please.

a jazz club	**un club de jazz** *oon kloob deh jazz*
a club with Spanish music	**un bar con música española** *oon bahr kohn moo·see·kah ehs·pah·nyoh·lah*
Is there live music?	**¿Hay música en vivo?** *aye moo·see·kah ehn bee·boh*
How do I get there?	**¿Cómo se llega allí?** *koh·moh seh yeh·gah ah·yee*
Is there a cover charge?	**¿Hay que pagar entrada?** *aye keh pah·gahr ehn·trah·dah*
Let's go dancing.	**Vamos a bailar.** *bah·mohs ah bayee·lahr*
Is this area safe at night?	**¿Esta zona es segura por la noche?** *ehs·tah tho·nah ehs seh·goo·rah pohr lah noh·cheh*

One of Spain's greatest cultural achievements is the **flamenco**. A combination of music, song and dance, the **flamenco** is an emotional performance that should not be missed when you are in Spain. Major cities such as Madrid, Seville and other Andalucian towns have **flamenco** performances year round. A **peña** is a small, intimate membership club (some allow guests) where you can view **flamenco** performed. **Tablaos** are typical public venues for **flamenco**. Seeing **flamenco** at a **tablao** can be an expensive night out, but well worth the money.

Special Requirements

Business Travel

ESSENTIAL

I'm here on business.	**Estoy aquí en viaje de negocios.** *ehs·toy ah·kee ehn beeyah·kheh deh neh·goh·theeyohs*
Here's my business card.	**Aquí tiene mi tarjeta.** *ah·kee teeyeh·neh mee tahr·kheh·tah*
Can I have your card?	**¿Puede darme su tarjeta?** *pweh·deh dahr·meh soo tahr·kheh·tah*
I have a meeting with...	**Tengo una reunión con...** *tehn·goh oo·nah rewoo·neeyohn kohn...*
Where's...?	**¿Dónde está...?** *dohn·deh ehs·tah...*
the business center	**el centro de negocios** *ehl thehn·troh deh neh·goh·theeyohs*
the convention hall	**el salón de congresos** *ehl sah·lohn deh kohn·greh·sohs*
the meeting room	**la sala de reuniones** *lah sah·lah deh rewoo·neeyohn·ehs*

On Business

I'm here to attend...	**Estoy aquí para asistir...** *ehs·toy ah·kee pah·rah ah·sees·teer...*
a seminar	**a un seminario** *ah oon seh·mee·nah·reeyoh*
a conference	**a una conferencia** *ah oo·nah kohn·feh·rehn·theeyah*
a meeting	**a una reunión** *ah oo·nah rewoo·neeyohn*
My name is...	**Me llamo...** *meh yah·moh...*
May I introduce my colleague...	**Le presento a mi compañero m/compañera f de trabajo...** *leh preh·sehn·toh ah mee kohm·pah·nyeh·roh/kohm·pah·nyeh·rah deh trah·bah·khoh...*

142

I have a meeting/an appointment with…	**Tengo una reunión/cita con…** *tehn•goh oo•nah rewoo•neeyohn/thee•tah kohn…*
I'm sorry I'm late.	**Perdone que haya llegado tarde.** *pehr•doh•neh keh ah•yah yeh•gah•doh tahr•deh*
I need an interpreter.	**Necesito un intérprete.** *neh•theh•see•toh oon een•tehr•preh•teh*
You can contact me at the…Hotel.	**Puede contactarme en el Hotel…** *pweh•deh kohn•tahk•tahr•meh ehn ehl oh•tehl…*
I'm here until…	**Estaré aquí hasta…** *ehs•tah•reh ah•kee ahs•tah…*
I need to…	**Necesito…** *neh•theh•see•toh…*
make a call	**hacer una llamada** *ah•thehr oo•nah yah•mah•dah*
make a photocopy	**hacer una fotocopia** *ah•thehr oo•nah foh•toh•koh•peeyah*
send an e-mail	**enviar un correo electrónico** *ehn•beeyahr oon koh•rreh•oh ee•lehk•troh•nee•koh*
send a fax	**enviar un fax** *ehn•beeyahr oon fahx*
send a package (for next-day delivery)	**enviar un paquete (para entrega el día siguiente)** *ehn•beeyahr oon pah•keh•teh (pah•rah ehn•treh•gah ehl dee•ah see•geeyehn•teh)*
It was a pleasure to meet you.	**Ha sido un placer conocerle *m*/conocerla *f*.** *ah see•doh oon plah•thehr koh•noh•thehr•leh/ koh•noh•thehr•lah*

For Communications, see page 49.

It is common to greet colleagues with **buenos días** (good day). Shake hands if it is the first time you are meeting someone in a professional setting, or if it is someone you haven't seen in a while. When leaving, simply say **adiós, gracias** (goodbye, thank you).

YOU MAY HEAR...

¿Tiene cita? _teeyeh·neh thee·tah_ Do you have an appointment?

¿Con quién? _kohn keeyehn_ With whom?

Está en una reunión. He/She is in a meeting.
ehs·tah ehn oo·nah rewoo·neeyohn

Un momento, por favor. One moment, please.
oon moh·mehn·toh pohr fah·bohr

Siéntese. _theeyehn·teh·seh_ Have a seat.

¿Quiere algo de beber? _keeyeh·reh_ Would you like something to drink?
ahl·goh deh beh·behr

Gracias por su visita. _grah·theeyahs_ Thank you for coming.
pohr soo bee·see·tah

Traveling with Children

ESSENTIAL

Is there a discount for kids?	**¿Hacen descuento a niños?** _ah·then dehs·kwehn·toh ah nee·nyohs_
Can you recommend a babysitter?	**¿Puede recomendarme una canguro?** _pweh·deh reh·koh·mehn·dahr·meh oo·nah kahn·goo·roh_
Do you have a child's seat/highchair?	**¿Tienen una silla para niños/trona?** _teeyeh·nehn oo·nah see·yah pah·rah nee·nyohs/troh·nah_
Where can I change the baby?	**¿Dónde puedo cambiar al bebé?** _dohn·deh pweh·doh kahm·beeyahr ahl beh·beh_

Out & About

Can you recommend something for kids?	**¿Puede recomendarme algo para los niños?** _pweh·deh reh·koh·mehn·dahr·meh ahl·goh pah·rah lohs nee·nyohs_
Where's…?	**¿Dónde está…?** _dohn·deh ehs·tah…_
the amusement park	**el parque de atracciones** _ehl pahr·keh deh ah·trahk·theeyoh·nehs_
the arcade	**el salón de juegos recreativos** _ehl sah·lohn deh khweh·gohs reh·kreh·ah·tee·bohs_
the kiddie [paddling] pool	**la piscina infantil** _lah pees·thee·nah een·fahn·teel_
the park	**el parque** _ehl pahr·keh_
the playground	**el parque infantil** _ehl pahr·keh een·fahn·teel_
the zoo	**el zoológico** _ehl thoh·oh·loh·khee·koh_
Are kids allowed?	**¿Se permite la entrada a niños?** _she pehr·mee·teh lah ehn·trah·dah ah nee·nyohs_
Is it safe for kids?	**¿Es seguro para niños?** _ehs seh·goo·roh pah·rah nee·nyohs_
Is it suitable for… year olds?	**¿Es apto para niños de…años?** _ehs ahp·toh pah·rah nee·nyohs deh…ah·nyohs_

For Numbers, see page 167.

YOU MAY HEAR…

¡Qué mono m/mona f! _keh moh·noh/moh·nah_	How cute!
¿Cómo se llama? _koh·moh seh yah·mah_	What's his/her name?
¿Qué edad tiene? _keh eh·dahth teeyeh·neh_	How old is he/she?

Baby Essentials

Do you have…?	**¿Tiene…?** _teeyeh·neh…_
a baby bottle	**un biberón** _oon bee·beh·rohn_
baby food	**la papilla** _lah papeeyah_
baby wipes	**toallitas** _toh·ah·yee·tahs_
a car seat	**un asiento para niños** _oon ah·seeyehn toh pah·rah nee·nyohs_
a children's menu/portion	**un menú/una ración para niños** _oon meh·noo/ oo·nah rah·theeyohn pah·rah nee·nyohs_
a child's seat/ highchair	**una silla para niños/trona** _oo·nah see·yah pah·rah nee·nyohs/troh·nah_
a crib/cot	**una cuna/un catre** _oo·nah koo·nah/oon kah·treh_
diapers [nappies]	**pañales** _pah·nyah·lehs_
formula	**fórmula infantil** _fohr·moo·lah een·fahn·teel_
a pacifier [dummy]	**un chupete** _oon choo·peh·teh_
a playpen	**un parque** _oon pahr·keh_
a stroller [pushchair]	**un cochecito** _oon koh·cheh·thee·toh_
Can I breastfeed the baby here?	**¿Puedo darle el pecho al bebé aquí?** _pweh·doh dahr·leh ehl peh·choh ahl beh·beh ah·kee_
Where can I change the baby?	**¿Dónde puedo cambiar al bebé?** _dohn·deh pweh·doh kahm·beeyahr ahl beh·beh_

Babysitting

Can you recommend a babysitter?	**¿Puede recomendarme una canguro?** _pweh·deh reh·koh·mehn·dahr·meh oo·nah kahn·goo·roh_
How much do they charge?	**¿Cuánto cuesta?** _kwahn·toh kwehs·tah_
I'll be back by…	**Vuelvo a la/las…** _bwehl·boh ah lah/lahs…_
If you need to contact me, call…	**Puede contactarme en el…** _pweh·deh kohn·tahk·tahr·meh ehn ehl…_

For Grammar, see page 162.

Health & Emergency

Can you recommend a pediatrician?	**¿Puede recomendarme un pediatra?** _pweh·deh reh·koh·mehn·<u>dahr</u>·meh oon peh·<u>deeyah</u>·trah_
My child is allergic to...	**Mi hijo** _m_/**hija** _f_ **es alérgico** _m_/**alérgica** _f_ **a...** _mee ee·khoh/ee·khah ehs ah·<u>lehr</u>·khee·koh/ ah·<u>lehr</u>·khee·kah ah..._
My child is missing.	**Mi hijo** _m_/**hija** _f_ **ha desaparecido.** _mee ee·khoh/ ee·khah ah deh·sah·pah·reh·<u>thee</u>·doh_
Have you seen a boy/girl?	**¿Ha visto a un niño** _m_/**una niña** _f_ **?** _ah <u>bees</u>·toh ah oon <u>nee</u>·nyoh/<u>oo</u>·nah <u>nee</u>·nyah_

Disabled Travelers

ESSENTIAL

Is there...?	**¿Hay...?** _aye..._
access for the disabled	**acceso para los discapacitados** _ahk·<u>theh</u>·soh pah·rah lohs dees·kah·pah·thee·<u>tah</u>·dohs_
a wheelchair ramp	**una rampa para sillas de ruedas** _oo·nah <u>rahm</u>·pah pah·rah <u>see</u>·yahs deh <u>rweh</u>·dahs_

a disabled-accessible toilet	**un baño con acceso para discapacitados** *oon bah·nyoh kohn ahk·theh·soh pah·rah dees·kah·pah·th/ee·tah·dohs*
I need...	**Necesito...** *neh·theh·see·toh...*
assistance	**ayuda** *ah·yoo·dah*
an elevator [a lift]	**un ascensor** *oon ahs·thehn·sohr*
a ground-floor room	**una habitación en la planta baja** *oo·nah ah·bee·tah·theeyohn ehn lah plahn·tah bah·khah*

Asking for Assistance

I'm disabled.	**Soy discapacitado m/discapacitada f** *soy dees·kah·pah·thee·tah·doh/ dees·kah·pah·thee·tah·dah*
I'm deaf.	**Soy sordo m/sorda f.** *soy sohr·doh/sohr·dah*
I'm visually/hearing impaired.	**Tengo discapacidad visual/auditiva.** *tehn·goh dees·kah·pah·thee·dahd bee·swahl/ awoo·dee·tee·bah*
I'm unable to walk far/use the stairs.	**No puedo caminar muy lejos/subir las escaleras.** *noh pweh·doh kah·mee·nahr mooy leh·khohs/ soo·beer lahs ehs·kah·leh·rahs*
Can I bring my wheelchair?	**¿Puedo traer la silla de ruedas?** *pweh·doh trah·ehr lah see·yah deh rweh·dahs*
Are guide dogs permitted?	**¿Permiten a perros guía?** *pehr·mee·tehn ah peh·rrohs gee·ah*
Can you help me?	**¿Puede ayudarme?** *pweh·deh ah·yoo·dahr·meh*
Please open/hold the door.	**Por favor, abra/aguante la puerta.** *pohr fah·bohr ah·brah/ah·gwahn·teh lah pwehr·tah*

In an
Emergency

Emergencies

ESSENTIAL

Help!	**¡Socorro!**	soh·koh·rroh
Go away!	**¡Lárguese!**	lahr·geh·seh
Stop, thief!	**¡Deténgase, ladrón!**	deh·tehn·gah·seh lah·drohn
Get a doctor!	**¡Llame a un médico!**	yah·meh ah oon meh·dee·koh
Fire!	**¡Fuego!**	fweh·goh
I'm lost.	**Me he perdido.**	meh eh pehr·dee·doh
Can you help me?	**¿Puede ayudarme?**	pweh·deh ah·yoo·dahr·meh

In an emergency, dial: **112** for the police
080 for the fire brigade
061 for the ambulance.

YOU MAY HEAR...

Rellene este impreso. reh·yeh·neh ehs·teh eem·preh·soh — Fill out this form.

Su documento de identidad, por favor. soo doh·koo·mehn·toh deh ee·dehn·tee·dahd pohr fah·bohr — Your identification, please.

¿Cuándo/Dónde ocurrió? kwahn·doh/dohn·deh oh·koo·rreeyoh — When/Where did it happen?

¿Puede describirle?/describirla? pweh·deh dehs·kree·beer·leh?/dehs·kree·beer·lah? — What does he/she look like?

Police

ESSENTIAL

Call the police!	**¡Llame a la policía!** _yah_•meh ah lah poh•lee•_thee_•ah
Where's the police station?	**¿Dónde está la comisaría?** _dohn_•deh ehs•_tah_ lah koh•mee•sah•_ree_•ah
There was an accident/attack.	**Ha habido un accidente/asalto.** ah ah•_bee_•doh oon ahk•thee•_dehn_•teh/ah•_sahl_•toh
My son/daughter is missing.	**Mi hijo m/hija f ha desaparecido.** mee ee•_khoh_/ ee•khah ah deh•sah•pah•reh•_thee_•doh
I need...	**Necesito...** neh•theh•_see_•toh...
an interpreter	**un intérprete** oon een•_tehr_•preh•teh
to contact my lawyer	**ponerme en contacto con mi abogado** poh•_nehr_•meh ehn kohn•_tahk_•toh kohn mee ah•boh•_gah_•doh
to make a phone call	**hacer una llamada** ah•_thehr_ _oo_•nah yah•_mah_•dah
I'm innocent.	**Soy inocente.** soy ee•noh•_thehn_•teh

Crime & Lost Property

I'd like to report...	**Quiero denunciar...** _keeyeh_•roh deh•noon•_theeyahr_...
a mugging	**un asalto** oon ah•_sahl_•toh
a rape	**una violación** _oo_•nah beeyoh•lah•_theeyohn_
a theft	**un robo** oon _roh_•boh
I've been mugged/robbed.	**Me han asaltado/atracado.** meh ahn ah•sahl•_tah_•doh/ah•trah•_kah_•doh
I've lost my...	**He perdido...** eh pehr•_dee_•doh...
My...was stolen.	**Me han robado...** meh ahn•roh•_bah_•doh...
backpack	**la mochila** lah moh•_chee_•lah
bicycle	**la bicicleta** lah bee•thee•_kleh_•tah

camera	**la cámara** *lah kah·mah·rah*
(hire) car	**el coche (de alquiler)** *ehl koh·cheh (deh ahl·kee·lehr)*
computer	**el ordenador** *ehl ohr·deh·nah·dohr*
credit card	**la tarjeta de crédito** *lah tahr·kheh·tah deh kreh·dee·toh*
jewelry	**las joyas** *lahs khoh·yahs*
money	**el dinero** *ehl dee·neh·roh*
passport	**el pasaporte** *ehl pah·sah·pohr·teh*
purse [handbag]	**el bolso** *ehl bohl·soh*
traveler's cheques	**los cheques de viaje** *lohs cheh·kehs deh beeyah·kheh*
wallet	**la cartera** *lah kahr·teh·rah*
I need a police report.	**Necesito un certificado de la policía.** *neh·theh·see·toh oon thehr·tee·fee·kah·doh deh lah poh·lee·thee·ah*
Where is the British/ American/Irish embassy?	**¿Dónde está la embajada británica/americana/ irlandesa?** *dohn·deh ehs·tah lah ehm·bah·khah·dah bree·tah·nee·kah/ah·meh·ree·kah·nah/eer·lahn·deh·sah*

ESSENTIAL

I'm sick [ill].	**Me encuentro mal.** meh ehn·<u>kwehn</u>·troh mahl
I need an English-speaking doctor.	**Necesito un médico que hable inglés.** neh·theh·<u>see</u>·toh oon <u>meh</u>·dee·koh keh <u>ah</u>·bleh een·<u>glehs</u>
It hurts here.	**Me duele aquí.** meh <u>dweh</u>·leh ah·<u>kee</u>
I have a stomachache.	**Tengo dolor de estómago.** <u>tehn</u>·goh doh·<u>lohr</u> deh ehs·<u>toh</u>·mah·goh

Finding a Doctor

Can you recommend a doctor/dentist?	**¿Puede recomendarme un médico/dentista?** <u>pweh</u>·deh reh·koh·mehn·<u>dahr</u>·meh oon <u>meh</u>·dee·koh/dehn·<u>tees</u>·tah
Can the doctor come here?	**¿Podría el médico venir aquí?** poh·<u>dree</u>·ah ehl <u>meh</u>·dee·koh beh·<u>neer</u> ah·<u>kee</u>
I need an English-speaking doctor.	**Necesito un médico que hable inglés.** neh·theh·<u>see</u>·toh oon <u>meh</u>·dee·koh keh <u>ah</u>·bleh een·<u>glehs</u>
What are the office hours?	**¿Cuáles son las horas de consulta?** <u>kwah</u>·lehs sohn lahs <u>oh</u>·rahs deh kohn·<u>sool</u>·tah
I'd like an appointment...	**Quiero una cita...** <u>keeyeh</u>·roh <u>oo</u>·nah <u>thee</u>·tah...
for today	**para hoy** <u>pah</u>·rah ohy
for tomorrow	**para mañana** <u>pah</u>·rah mah·<u>nyah</u>·nah
as soon as possible	**lo antes posible** loh <u>ahn</u>·tehs poh·<u>see</u>·bleh
It's urgent.	**Es urgente.** ehs oor·<u>khehn</u>·teh

Symptoms

I'm…	**Estoy…** *ehs•toy…*
bleeding	**sangrando** *sahn•grahn•doh*
constipated	**estreñido** *m*/**estreñida** *f ehs•treh•nyee•doh/* *ehs•treh•nyee•dah*
dizzy	**mareado** *m*/**mareada** *f mah•reh•ah•doh/* *mah•reh•ah•dah*
I'm nauseous	**Tengo náuseas.** *tehn•goh naw•seh•ahs*
I'm vomiting.	**Tengo vómitos.** *tehn•goh boh•mee•tohs*
It hurts here.	**Me duele aquí.** *meh dweh•leh ah•kee*
I have…	**Tengo…** *tehn•goh…*
an allergic reaction	**una reacción alérgica** *oo•nah reh•ahk•theeyohn ah•lehr•khee•kah*
chest pain	**dolor de pecho** *doh•lohr deh peh•choh*
cramps	**calambres** *kah•lahm•brehs*
diarrhea	**diarrea** *deeyah•rreh•ah*
an earache	**dolor de oído** *doh•lohr deh oh•ee•doh*
a fever	**fiebre** *feeyeh•breh*
pain	**dolor** *doh•lohr*
a rash	**una erupción cutánea** *oo•nah eh•roop•theeyohn koo•tah•nee•ah*
a sprain	**un esguince** *oon ehs•geen•theh*
some swelling	**una hinchazón** *oo•nah een•chah•thohn*
a stomachache	**dolor de estómago** *doh•lohr deh ehs•toh•mah•goh*
sunstroke	**una insolación** *oo•nah een•soh•lah•theeyohn*
I've been sick [ill] for…days.	**Llevo…días que me encuentro mal.** *yeh•boh…dee•ahs keh meh ehn•kwehn•troh mahl*

For Numbers, see page 167.

Conditions

I'm...	**Soy...** *soy...*
anemic	**anémico** *m*/**anémica** *f ah-neh-mee-koh/ ah-neh-mee-kah*
asthmatic	**asmático** *m*/**asmática** *f ahs-mah-tee-koh/ ahs-mah-tee-kah*
diabetic	**diabético** *m*/**diabética** *f deeyah-beh-tee-koh/ deeyah-beh-tee-kah*
epileptic	**epiléptico** *m*/**epileptica** *f eh-pee-lehp-tee-koh/ eh-pee-lehp-tee-kah*
I'm allergic to antibiotics/penicillin.	**Soy alérgico** *m*/**alérgica** *f* **a los antibióticos/ la penicilina.** *soy ah-lehr-khee-koh/ah-lehr-khee-kah ah lohs ahn-tee-beeyoh-tee-kohs/ lah peh-nee-thee-lee-nah*

YOU MAY HEAR...

¿Qué le pasa? *keh leh pah-sah*	What's wrong?
¿Dónde le duele? *dohn-deh leh dweh-leh*	Where does it hurt?
¿Le duele aquí? *leh dweh-leh ah-kee*	Does it hurt here?
¿Esta tomando algún medicamento? *ehs-tah toh-mahn-doh ahl-goon meh-dee-kah-mehn-toh*	Are you on medication?
¿Es alérgico *m*/**alérgica** *f* **a algo?** *ehs ah-lehr-khee-koh/ah-lehr-khee-kah ah ahl-goh*	Are you allergic to anything?
Abra la boca. *ah-brah lah boh-kah*	Open your mouth.
Respire hondo. *rehs-pee-reh ohn-doh*	Breathe deeply.
Tiene que ir al hospital. *teeyeh-neh keh eer ahl ohs-pee-tahl*	You/he/she must go to the hospital.

I have...	**Tengo...** _tehn_·goh
arthritis	**artritis** ahr·_tree_·tees
(high/low) blood pressure.	**la tensión (alta/baja).** lah tehn·_seeyohn_ (_ahl_·tah/_bah_·khah)
I have a heart condition.	**Padezco del corazón.** pah·_dehth_·koh dehl koh·rah·_thon_
I'm on...	**Estoy tomando...** ehs·_toy_ toh·_mahn_·doh...

For Meals & Cooking, see page 66.

Treatment

Do I need a prescription/ medicine?	**¿Necesito una receta/un medicamento?** neh·theh·_see_·toh _oo_·nah reh·_theh_·tah/ oon meh·dee·kah·_mehn_·toh
Can you prescribe a generic drug? [unbranded medication]?	**¿Puede recetarme un medicamento genérico?** pweh·deh reh·theh·tahr·meh oon meh·dee·kah·mehn·toh kheh·neh·ree·koh
Where can I get it?	**¿Dónde puedo conseguirlo?** dohn·de pweh·doh kohn·seh·geer·loh

For What to Take, see page 159.

Hospital

Notify my family, please.	**Por favor, avise a mi familia.** pohr fah·_bohr_ ah·_bee_·seh ah mee fah·_mee_·leeyah
I'm in pain.	**Tengo dolor.** _tehn_·goh doh·_lohr_
I need a doctor/nurse.	**Necesito un médico/una enfermera.** neh·thee·_see_·toh oon _meh_·dee·koh/_oo_·nah ehn·fehr·_meh_·rah
When are visiting hours?	**¿Qué horas de visita tienen?** keh _oh_·rahs deh bee·_see_·tah teeyeh·nehn
I'm visiting...	**Vengo a hacer una visita a...** _behn_·goh ah ah·_thehr_ _oo_·nah bee·_see_·tah ah...

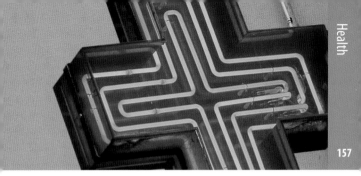

Dentist

I've broken a tooth/lost a filling.	**Se me ha roto un diente/caído un empaste.** *seh meh ah roh·toh oon deeyehn·teh/ kah·ee·doh oon ehm·pahs·teh*
I have a toothache.	**Tengo dolor de muelas.** *tehn·goh doh·lohr deh mweh·lahs*
Can you fix this denture?	**¿Puede arreglarme la dentadura postiza?** *pweh·deh ah·rreh·glahr·meh lah dehn·tah·doo·rah pohs·tee·thah*

Gynecologist

I have menstrual cramps/a vaginal infection.	**Tengo dolores menstruales/una infección vaginal.** *tehn·goh doh·loh·rehs mehns·trwah·lehs/ oo·nah een·fehk·theeyohn bah·khee·nahl*
I missed my period.	**No me ha venido la regla.** *noh meh ah beh·nee·doh lah reh·glah*
I'm on the Pill.	**Tomo la píldora.** *toh·moh lah peel·doh·rah*
I'm (… months) pregnant.	**Estoy embarazada (de… meses).** *esh·toy ehm·bah·rah·thah·dah (deh… meh·sehs)*
I'm not pregnant.	**No estoy embarazada.** *noh ehs·toy ehm·bah·rah·thah·dah*

My last period was…	**La última vez que me vino la regla fue…**
	lah ool·tee·mah behth keh meh bee·noh lah
	reh·glah fweh…

For Numbers see page 167.

Optician

I've lost…	**He perdido…** *eh pehr·dee·doh…*
a contact lens	**una lentilla** *oo·nah lehn·tee·yah*
my glasses	**las gafas** *lahs gah·fahs*
a lens	**una lente** *oo·nah lehn·teh*

Payment & Insurance

How much?	**¿Cuánto es?** *kwahn·toh ehs*
Can I pay by credit card?	**¿Puedo pagar con tarjeta de crédito?** *pweh·doh pah·gahr kohn tahr·kheh·tah deh kreh·dee·toh*
I have insurance.	**Tengo seguro médico.** *tehn·goh seh·goo·roh meh·dee·koh*
I need a receipt for my insurance.	**Necesito una factura para el seguro médico.** *neh·theh·see·toh oo·nah fahk·too·rah pah·rah ehl seh·goo·roh meh·dee·koh*

Pharmacy

ESSENTIAL

Where's the pharmacy?	**¿Dónde está la farmacia?** *dohn·deh ehs·tah lah fahr·mah·theeyah*
What time does it open/close?	**¿A qué hora abre/cierra?** *ah keh oh·rah ah·breh/theeyeh·rrah*
What would you recommend for…?	**¿Qué me recomienda para…?** *keh meh reh·koh·meeyehn·dah pah·rah…*

158

How much do I take?	**¿Qué dosis me tomo?** *keh doh•sees meh toh•moh*
Can you fill [make up] this prescription?	**¿Puede darme este medicamento?** *pweh•deh dahr•meh ehs•the meh•dee•kah•mehn•toh*
I'm allergic to...	**Soy alérgico *m*/alérgica *f* a...** *soy ah•lehr•khee•koh/ah•lehr•khee•kah ah...*

Pharmacies are easily identified by their green neon signs in the shape of a cross. Opening hours are generally from 9:00 a.m. until 1:30 p.m., closed for **siesta** in teh afternoon and then open from 4:30 p.m. until 8:00 p.m. There are 24-hour pharmacies available in larger cities. A list of pharmacies that are open at night or on weekends can be found in the windows of all pharmacies, and the list is also published in the local newspapers.

What to Take

How much do I take?	**¿Qué dosis me tomo?** *keh doh•sees meh toh•moh*
How often?	**¿Con qué frecuencia?** *kohn keh freh•kwehn•theeyah*
Is it safe for children?	**¿Está indicado para niños?** *ehs•tah een•dee•kah•doh pah•rah nee•nyohs*
I'm taking...	**Estoy tomando...** *ehs•toy toh•mahn•doh...*
Are there side effects?	**¿Tiene algún efecto secundario?** *teeyeh•neh ahl•goon eh•fehk•toh seh•koon•dah•reeyoh*
I need something for...	**Necesito algo para...** *neh•theh•see•toh ahl•goh pah•rah...*
a cold	**el catarro** *ehl kah•tah•rroh*
a cough	**la tos** *lah tohs*
diarrhea	**la diarrea** *lah deeyah•rreh•ah*

a headache	**el dolor de cabeza** *ehl doh·lohr deh kah·beh·thah*
insect bites	**las picaduras de insecto** *lahs pee·kah·doo·rahs deh een·sehk·toh*
motion [travel] sickness	**la cinetosis** *lah thee·neh·toh·sees*
a sore throat	**las anginas** *lahs ahn·khee·nahs*
sunburn	**la quemadura solar** *lah keh·mah·doo·rah soh·lahr*
a toothache	**el dolor de muelas** *ehl doh·lohr deh moo·eh·lahs*
an upset stomach	**el malestar estomacal** *ehl mah·lehs·tahr ehs·toh·mah·kahl*

YOU MAY SEE...

UNA VEZ/TRES VECES AL DÍA	once/three times a day
COMPRIMIDO	tablet
GOTA	drop
CUCHARADITA	teaspoon
DESPUÉS DE/ANTES DE/CON LAS COMIDAS	after/before/with meals
CON EL ESTÓMAGO VACÍO	on an empty stomach
TRAGUE EL COMPRIMIDO ENTERO	swallow whole
PUEDE CAUSAR SOMNOLENCIA	may cause drowsiness
DE USO TÓPICO SOLAMENTE	for external use only

Basic Supplies

I'd like...	**Quiero...** *keeyeh·roh...*
acetaminophen [paracetamol]	**paracetamol** *pah·rah·thee·tah·mohl*
antiseptic cream	**crema antiséptica** *kreh·mah ahn·tee·sehp·tee·kah*
aspirin	**aspirinas** *ahs·pee·ree·nahs*
bandages	**tiritas** *tee·ree·tahs*

a comb	**un peine** oon _peyee_•neh
condoms	**preservativos** preh•sehr•bah•_tee_•bohs
contact lens	**líquido de lentillas** _lee_•kee•doh deh
solution	lehn•_tee_•yahs
deodorant	**desodorante** deh•soh•doh•_rahn_•teh
a hairbrush	**un cepillo de pelo** oon theh•_pee_•yoh deh _peh_•loh
hairspray	**laca** lah•kah
ibuprofen	**ibuprofeno** ee•boo•proh•_feh_•noh
insect repellent	**repelente de insectos** reh•peh•_lehn_•the
	deh een•_sehk_•tohs
lotion	**crema hidratante** _kreh_•mah ee•drah•_tahn_•teh
a nail file	**una lima de uñas** oo•nah lee•mah deh oo•nyahs
a (disposable) razor	**una cuchilla** _oo_•nah koo•_chee_•yah
razor blades	**hojas de afeitar** _oh_•khahs deh ah•feyee•_tahr_
sanitary napkins [towels]	**compresas** kohm•_preh_•sahs
shampoo/	**champú/suavizante** chahm•_poo_/
conditioner	swah•bee•_thahn_•teh
soap	**jabón** khah•_bohn_
sunscreen	**protector solar** proh•tehk•_tohr_ soh•_lahr_
tampons	**tampones** tahm•_poh_•nehs
tissues	**pañuelos de papel** pah•_nyweh_•lohs deh pah•_pehl_
toilet paper	**papel higiénico** pah•_pehl_ ee•_kheeyeh_•nee•koh
a toothbrush	**un cepillo de dientes** oon theh•_pee_•yoh
	deh _deeyehn_•tehs
toothpaste	**pasta de dientes** _pahs_•tah deh _deeyehn_•tehs

For Baby Essentials, see page 146.

The Basics

Grammar

In Spanish, there are a number of forms for 'you' (taking different verb forms): **tú** (singular) and **vosotros** *m*/**vosotras** *f* (plural) are used when talking to relatives, close friends and children; **usted** (singular) and **ustedes** (plural) are used in all other cases. If in doubt, use **usted/ustedes**. The following abbreviations are used in this section: Ud. = Usted; Uds. = Ustedes; sing. = singular; pl. = plural; inf. = informal; for. = formal.

Regular Verbs

There are three verb types that follow a regular conjugation pattern. These verbs end in **–ar**, **–er** and **–ir**. Following are the present, past and future forms of the verbs **hablar** (to speak), **comer** (to eat) and **vivir** (to live). The different conjugation endings are in bold.

HABLAR		Present	Past	Future
I	**yo**	habl**o**	habl**é**	habl**aré**
you (sing.)	**tú**	habl**as**	habl**aste**	habl**arás**
he/she/you	**él/ella/Ud.**	habl**a**	habl**ó**	habl**ará**
we	**nosotros**	habl**amos**	habl**amos**	habl**aremos**
you (pl.)	**vosotros** *m* **vosotras** *f*	habl**áis**	habl**asteis**	habl**aréis**
they/you	**ellos/ellas/ Uds.**	habl**an**	habl**aron**	habl**arán**

COMER		Present	Past	Future
I	**yo**	com**o**	com**í**	com**eré**
you (sing.)	**tú**	com**es**	com**iste**	com**erás**
he/she/you	**él/ella/Ud.**	com**e**	com**ió**	com**erá**
we	**nosotros**	com**emos**	com**imos**	com**eremos**

you (pl.)	**vosotros** *m*	com**éis**	com**isteis**	com**eréis**
	vosotras *f*			
they/you	**ellos/ellas/**	com**en**	com**ieron**	com**erán**
	Uds.			

VIVIR		Present	Past	Future
I	**yo**	viv**o**	viv**í**	viv**iré**
you (sing.)	**tú**	viv**es**	viv**iste**	viv**irás**
he/she/you	**él/ella/Ud.**	viv**e**	viv**ió**	viv**irá**
we	**nosotros**	viv**imos**	viv**imos**	viv**iremos**
you (pl.)	**vosotros** *m*	viv**ís**	viv**isteis**	viv**iréis**
	vosotras *f*			
they/you	**ellos/ellas/**	viv**en**	viv**ieron**	viv**irán**
	Uds.			

Irregular Verbs

In Spanish, there are many different irregular verbs; these aren't conjugated by following the normal rules. The two most commonly used, and confused, irregular verbs are **ser** and **estar**. Both verbs mean 'to be', but are used in different contexts (see page 164). Following is the past, present and future tenses of **ser** and **estar** for easy reference.

SER	Present	Past	Future
yo	soy	fui	seré
tú (sing.)	eres	fuiste	serás
él/ella/Ud.	es	fue	será
nosotros	somos	fuimos	seremos
vosotros *m*	sois	fuisteis	seréis
vosotras *f* (pl.)			
ellos/ellas/Uds.	son	fueron	serán

ESTAR	Present	Past	Future
yo	estoy	estuve	estaré
tú (sing.)	estás	estuviste	estarás
él/ella/Ud.	está	estuvo	estará
nosotros	estamos	estuvimos	estaremos
vosotros *m* **vosotras** *f* (pl.)	estáis	estuvisteis	estaréis
ellos/ellas/Uds.	están	estuvieron	estarán

Ser is used to describe a fixed quality or characteristic. It is also used to tell time and dates. Example: **Yo soy estadounidense.** I am American.

Here **ser** is used because it is a permanent characteristic.

Estar is used when describing a physical location or a temporary condition. Example: **Estoy cansado.** I am tired.

Here **estar** is used because being tired is a temporary condition.

Word Order

In Spanish, the conjugated verb comes after the subject.

Example: **Yo trabajo en Madrid.** I work in Madrid.

To ask a question, reverse the order of the subject and verb, change your intonation or use key question words such as **cuándo** (when).

Examples: **¿Cuándo cierra el banco?** When does the bank close?

Literally translates to: 'When closes the bank?' Notice the order of the subject and verb is reversed; a question word also begins the sentence.

¿El hotel es viejo? Is the hotel old?

Literally, the hotel is old. This is a statement that becomes a question by raising the pitch of the last syllable of the sentence.

Negations

To form a negative sentence, add **no** (not) before the verb.

Example: **Fumamos.** We smoke.

No fumamos. We don't smoke.

Imperatives

Imperative sentences, or sentences that are a command, are formed by adding the appropriate ending to the stem of the verb (i.e. the verb in the infinitive without the **-ar**, **-er**, **-ir** ending). Example: Speak!

you (sing.) (inf.)	tú	**¡Habla!**
you (sing.) (for.)	Ud.	**¡Hable!**
we	nosotros	**¡Hablemos!**
you (inf.)	vosotros	**¡Hablad!**
you (pl.) (for.)	Uds.	**¡Hablen!**

Nouns & Articles

Nouns are either masculine or feminine. Masculine nouns usually end in **–o**, and feminine nouns usually end in **–a**. Nouns become plural by adding an **–s**, or **–es** to nouns not ending in **–o** or **–a** (e.g. **tren** becomes **trenes**). Nouns in Spanish get an indefinite or definite article. An article must agree with the noun to which it refers in gender and number. Indefinite articles are the equivalent of 'a', 'an' or 'some' in English, while definite articles are the equivalent of 'the'.

Indefinite article examples: **un tren** *m* (a train); **unos trenes** *m* (some trains)**; una mesa** *f* (a table); **unas mesas** *f* (some tables)

Definite examples: **el libro** *m* (the book); **los libros** *m* (the books); **la casa** *f* (the house); **las casas** *f* (the houses)

A possessive adjective relates to the gender of the noun that follows and must agree in number and gender.

	Singular	Plural
my	**mi**	**mis**
your (sing.)	**tu**	**tus**
his/her/its/your	**su**	**sus**
our	**nuestro** *m* /**nuestra** *f*	**nuestros** *m* /**nuestras** *f*
your (pl.)	**vuestro** *m* /**vuestra** *f*	**vuestros** *m* /**vuestras** *f*
their/your	**su**	**sus**

Examples: **¿Dónde está <u>tu</u> chaqueta?** Where is your jacket?
<u>Vuestro</u> vuelo sale a las ocho. Your flight leaves at eight.

Adjectives

Adjectives describe nouns and must agree with the noun in gender and
number. In Spanish, adjectives usually come after the noun. Masculine
adjectives generally end in **–o**, feminine adjectives in **–a**. If the masculine
form ends in **–e** or with a consonant, the feminine form is generally the same.
Most adjectives form their plurals the same way as nouns.

Examples: **Su hijo** m/**hija** f **es simpatico** m/**simpatico** f. Your son/daughter
is nice.

El mar m/**La flor** f **es azul.** The ocean/The flower is blue.

Comparatives & Superlatives

The comparative is usually formed by adding **más** (more) or **menos** (less)
before the adjective or noun. The superlative is formed by adding the
appropriate definite article (**la/las**, **el/los**) and **más** (the most) **menos** (the
least) before the adjective or noun. Example:

grande	**más grande**	**el** m/**la** f **más grande**
big	bigger	biggest
caro m/**cara** f	**menos caro** m/**cara** f	**el** m/**la** f **menos caro** m/**cara** f
expensive	less expensive	least expensive

Possessive Pronouns

Pronouns serve as substitutes for specific nouns and must agree with the noun
in gender and number.

	Singular	Plural
mine	**mío** m/**mía** f	**míos** m/**mías** f
yours (inf.)	**tuyo** m/**tuya** f	**tuyos** m/**tuyas** f
yours	**suyo** m/**suya** f	**suyos** m/**suyas** f

his/her/its	**suyo** m/**suya** f	**suyos** m/**suyas** f
ours	**nuestro** m/**nuestra** f	**nuestros** m/**nuestras** f
yours (inf.)	**vuestro** m/**vuestra** f	**vuestros** m/**vuestras** f
theirs	**suyo** m/**suya** f	**suyos** m/**suyas** f

Example: **Ese asiento es mío.** That seat is mine.

Adverbs & Adverbial Expressions

Adverbs are used to describe verbs. Some adverbs are formed by adding -**mente** to the adjective.

Example: **Roberto conduce lentamente.** Robert drives slowly.

The following are some common adverbial time expressions:

actualmente presently

todavía no not yet

todavía still

ya no not anymore

Numbers

ESSENTIAL

0	**cero** _theh•roh_
1	**uno** _oo•noh_
2	**dos** _dohs_
3	**tres** _trehs_
4	**cuatro** _kwah•troh_
5	**cinco** _theen•koh_
6	**seis** _seyees_
7	**siete** _seeyeh•teh_
8	**ocho** _oh•choh_
9	**nueve** _nweh•beh_
10	**diez** _deeyehth_

11	**once** _ohn_·theh
12	**doce** _doh_·theh
13	**trece** _treh_·theh
14	**catorce** kah·_tohr_·theh
15	**quince** _keen_·theh
16	**dieciséis** deeyeh·thee·_seyees_
17	**diecisiete** deeyeh·thee·_seeyeh_·teh
18	**dieciocho** deeyeh·thee·_oh_·choh
19	**diecinueve** deeyeh·thee·_nweh_·beh
20	**veinte** _beyeen_·teh
21	**veintiuno** beyeen·tee·_oo_·noh
22	**veintidós** beyeen·tee·_dohs_
30	**treinta** _treyeen_·tah
31	**treinta y uno** _treyeen_·tah ee _oo_·noh
40	**cuarenta** kwah·_rehn_·tah
50	**cincuenta** theen·_kwehn_·tah
60	**sesenta** seh·_sehn_·tah
70	**setenta** seh·_tehn_·tah
80	**ochenta** oh·_chehn_·tah
90	**noventa** noh·_behn_·tah
100	**cien** theeyehn
101	**ciento uno** _theeyehn_·toh _oo_·noh
200	**doscientos** dohs·_theeyehn_·tohs
500	**quinientos** kee·_neeyehn_·tohs
1,000	**mil** meel
10,000	**diez mil** deeyehht meel
1,000,000	**un millón** oon mee·_yohn_

Large numbers are read as in English. Example: 1,234,567 would be **un millón, doscientos treinta y cuatro mil, quinientos sesenta y siete** (one million, two hundred thirty-four thousand, five hundred sixty-seven). Notice the use of **y** (and) between tens and units for numbers between 31 (**treinta y uno**; literally, thirty and one) and 99 (**noventa y nueve**; literally, ninety and nine).

Ordinal Numbers

first	**primero** m/**primera** f pree·_meh_·roh/pree·_meh_·rah
second	**segundo** m/**segunda** f seh·_goon_·doh/seh·_goon_·dah
third	**tercero** m/**tercera** f tehr·_theh_·roh/tehr·_theh_·rah
fourth	**cuarto** m/**cuarta** f _kwahr_·toh/_kwahr_·tah
fifth	**quinto** m/**quinta** f _keen_·toh/_keen_·tah
once	**una vez** _oo_·nah behth
twice	**dos veces** dohs _beh_·thes
three times	**tres veces** trehs _beh_·thes

Time

ESSENTIAL

What time is it?	**¿Qué hora es?** *keh <u>oh</u>•rah ehs*
It's noon [midday].	**Son las doce del mediodía.** *sohn lahs <u>doh</u>•theh dehl meh•deeyoh•<u>dee</u>•ah*
At midnight.	**A medianoche.** *ah meh•deeyah•<u>noh</u>•cheh*
From one o'clock to two o'clock.	**De una a dos en punto.** *deh <u>oo</u>•nah ah dohs ehn <u>poon</u>•toh*
Five after [past] three.	**Las tres y cinco.** *lahs trehs ee <u>theen</u>•koh*
A quarter to five.	**Las cinco menos cuarto.** *lahs <u>theen</u>•koh <u>meh</u>•nohs <u>kwahr</u>•toh*
5:30 a.m./p.m.	**Las cinco y media de la mañana/tarde.** *lahs <u>theen</u>•koh ee <u>meh</u>•deeyah deh lah mah•<u>nyah</u>•nah/<u>tahr</u>•deh*

Spaniards use the 24-hour clock when writing time, especially in schedules. The morning hours from 1:00 a.m. to noon are the same as in English. After that, just add 12 to the time: 1:00 p.m. would be 13:00, 5:00 p.m. would be 17:00 and so on.

Days

ESSENTIAL

Monday	**lunes** _loo_•nehs
Tuesday	**martes** _mahr_•tehs
Wednesday	**miércoles** _meeyehr_•koh•lehs
Thursday	**jueves** _khweh_•behs
Friday	**viernes** _beeyehr_•nehs
Saturday	**sábado** _sah_•bah•doh
Sunday	**domingo** doh•_meen_•goh

Dates

yesterday	**ayer** ah•_yehr_
today	**hoy** oy
tomorrow	**mañana** mah•_nyah_•nah
day	**día** _dee_•ah
week	**semana** seh•_mah_•nah
month	**mes** mehs
year	**año** _ah_•nyoh

Months

January	**enero** eh•_neh_•roh
February	**febrero** feh•_breh_•roh
March	**marzo** _mahr_•thoh
April	**abril** ah•_breel_
May	**mayo** _mah_•yoh
June	**junio** _khoo_•neeyoh
July	**julio** _khoo_•leeyoh
August	**agosto** ah•_gohs_•toh

Spain follows a day-month-year format instead of the month-day-year format favored in the U.S.
Examples: **el 25 de agosto de 2007** = August 25, 2007
25.8.07 = 8/25/2007

September	**septiembre** *sehp·teeyehm·breh*
October	**octubre** *ohk·too·breh*
November	**noviembre** *noh·beeyehm·breh*
December	**diciembre** *dee·theeyehm·breh*

Seasons

the spring	**la primavera** *lah pree·mah·beh·rah*
the summer	**el verano** *ehl beh·rah·noh*
the fall [autumn]	**el otoño** *ehl oh·toh·nyoh*
the winter	**el invierno** *ehl een·beeyehr·noh*

Holidays

January 1: New Year's Day, **Año Nuevo**
January 6: Epiphany, **Epifanía**
February 8: Carnaval, **Carnaval**
March 19: Feast of St. Joseph, **San José**
May 1: Labor Day, **Día del Trabajo**
July 25: Feast of St. James, **Santiago Apóstol**

In Spain, the week begins with Monday and ends on Sunday. This distinction is especially apparent when looking at calendars — Monday will be the first column instead of Sunday.

August 15: Feast of the Assumption, **Asunción**

October 12: Spain's National Day, **Día de la Hispanidad**

November 1: All Saint's Day, **Todos los Santos**

December 6: Constitution Day, **Día de la Constitución**

December 8: Feast of the Immaculate Conception, **Inmaculada Concepción**

December 25: Christmas, **Navidad**

Easter festivities take place on different dates each year since this holiday is traditionally celebrated on the first Sunday after the first full moon, on or after the spring equinox.

Conversion Tables

When you know	Multiply by	To find
ounces	28.3	grams
pounds	0.45	kilograms
inches	2.54	centimeters
feet	0.3	meters
miles	1.61	kilometers
square inches	6.45	sq. centimeters
square feet	0.09	sq. meters
square miles	2.59	sq. kilometers
pints (U.S./Brit)	0.47/0.56	liters
gallons (U.S./Brit)	3.8/4.5	liters
Fahrenheit	5/9, after −32	Centigrade
Centigrade	9/5, then +32	Fahrenheit

Kilometers to Miles Conversions

1 km – 0.62 mi	**20 km** – 12.4 mi
5 km – 3.10 mi	**50 km** – 31.0 mi
10 km – 6.20 mi	**100 km** – 61.0 mi

Measurement

1 gram	**un gramo** *oon grah·moh*	= 0.035 oz.
1 kilogram (kg)	**un kilogramo** *oon kee·loh·grah·moh*	= 2.2 lb
1 liter (l)	**un litro** *oon lee·troh*	= 1.06 U.S/0.88 Brit. quarts
1 centimeter (cm)	**un centímetro** *oon thehn·tee·meh·troh*	= 0.4 inch
1 meter (m)	**un metro** *oon meh·troh*	= 3.28 ft.
1 kilometer (km)	**un kilómetro** *oon kee·loh·meh·troh*	= 0.62 mile

Temperature

-40° C – -40° F	**-1**° C – 30° F	**20**° C – 68° F
-30° C – -22° F	**0**° C – 32° F	**25**° C – 77° F
-20° C – -4° F	**5**° C – 41° F	**30**° C – 86° F
-10° C – 14° F	**10**° C – 50° F	**35**° C – 95° F
-5° C – 23° F	**15**° C – 59° F	

Oven Temperature

100° C – 212° F	**177**° C – 350° F
121° C – 250° F	**204**° C – 400° F
149° C – 300° F	**260**° C – 500° F

Dictionary

gerundio m GRAM gerund
gestación f gestation
gesticular ⟨1a⟩ v/i gesticulate
gestión f management;
(trámites) formalities, procedure
⟨1a⟩ v/t trámites take

English–Spanish

A

abbey la abadía
accept v aceptar
access el acceso
accident el accidente
accommodation el alojamiento
account la cuenta
acupuncture la acupuntura
adapter el adaptador
address la dirección
admission la entrada
after después; ~**noon** la tarde;
  ~**shave** el bálsamo para después
  del afeitado
age la edad
agency la agencia
AIDS el sida
air el aire; ~ **conditioning**
  el aire acondicionado; ~
  pump el aire; ~**line** la compañía
  aérea; ~**mail** el correo aéreo;
  ~**plane** el avión; ~**port** el
  aeropuerto
aisle el pasillo; ~ **seat** el asiento
  de pasillo

allergic alérgico; ~ **reaction**
  la reacción alérgica
allow v permitir
alone solo
alter v **(clothing)** hacer un arreglo
alternate route el otro camino
aluminum foil el papel de aluminio
amazing increíble
ambulance la ambulancia
American estadounidense
amusement park el parque
  de atracciones
anemic anémico
anesthesia la anestesia
animal el animal
ankle el tobillo
antibiotic el antibiótico
antiques store la tienda de
  -antigüedades
antiseptic cream la crema
  antiséptica
anything algo
apartment el apartamento
appendix (body part) el apéndice
appetizer el aperitivo

| **adj** adjective | **BE** British English | **v** verb |
| **adv** adverb | **n** noun | |

appointment la cita
arcade el salón de juegos recreativos
area code el prefijo
arm el brazo
aromatherapy la aromaterapia
around (the corner) doblando (la esquina)
arrivals (airport) las llegadas
arrive v llegar
artery la arteria
arthritis la artritis
arts las letras
Asian asiático
aspirin la aspirina
asthmatic asmático
ATM el cajero automático
attack el asalto
attend v asistir
attraction (place) el sitio de interés
attractive guapo
Australia Australia
Australian australiano
automatic automático; **~ car** coche automático
available disponible

B

baby el bebé; **~ bottle** el biberón; **~ wipe** la toallita; **~sitter** el/la canguro

back la espalda; **~ache** el dolor de espalda; **~pack** la mochila
bag la maleta
baggage el equipaje; **~ claim** la recogida de equipajes; **~ ticket** el talón de equipaje
bakery la panadería
ballet el ballet
bandage la tirita
bank el banco
bar el bar
barbecue la barbacoa
barber la peluquería de caballeros
baseball el béisbol
basket (grocery store) la cesta
basketball el baloncesto
bathroom el baño
battery (car) la batería
battery la pila
battleground el campo de batalla
be v ser, estar
beach la playa
beautiful precioso
bed la cama; **~ and breakfast** la pensión
begin v empezar
before antes de
beginner principiante
behind detrás de
beige beis
belt el cinturón

berth la litera
best el/la mejor
better mejor
bicycle la bicicleta
big grande
bigger más grande
bike route el sendero para bicicletas
bikini el biquini;
  ~ **wax** la depilación de las ingles
bill v **(charge)** cobrar;
  ~n **(money)** el billete;
  ~n **(of sale)** el recibo
bird el pájaro
birthday el cumpleaños
black negro
bladder la vejiga
bland soso
blanket la manta
bleed v sangrar
blood la sangre; ~ **pressure** la tensión arterial
blouse la blusa
blue azul
board v embarcar
boarding pass la tarjeta de embarque
boat el barco
bone el hueso
book el libro; ~**store** la librería
boots las botas

boring aburrido
botanical garden el jardín botánico
bother v molestar
bottle la botella; ~ **opener** el abrebotellas
bowl el cuenco
box la caja
boxing match la pelea de boxeo
boy el niño; ~**friend** el novio
bra el sujetador
bracelet la pulsera
brakes (car) los frenos
break v romper
break-in (burglary) el allanamiento de morada
breakdown la avería
breakfast el desayuno
breast el seno; ~**feed** dar el pecho
breathe v respirar
bridge el puente
briefs (clothing) los calzoncillos
bring v traer
British británico
broken roto
brooch el broche
broom la escoba
brother el hermano
brown marrón
bug el insecto
building el edificio
burn v **(CD)** grabar

bus el autobús; **~ station** la estación de autobuses; **~ stop** la parada de autobús; **~ ticket** el billete de autobús; **~ tour** el recorrido en autobús

business los negocios; **~ card** la tarjeta de negocios; **~ center** el centro de negocios; **~ class** la clase preferente; **~ hours** el horario de atención al público

butcher el carnicero

buttocks las nalgas

buy *v* comprar

bye adiós

C

cabaret el cabaré

cabin (house) la cabaña; **~ (ship)** el camarote

cable car el teleférico

cafe la cafetería

call *v* llamar; **~** *n* la llamada

calories las calorías

camera la cámara; **digital ~** la cámara digital; **~ case** la funda para la cámara; **~ store** la tienda de fotografía

camp *v* acampar; **~ stove** el hornillo; **~site** el cámping

can opener el abrelatas

Canada Canadá

Canadian canadiense

cancel *v* cancelar

candy el caramelo

canned goods las conservas

canyon el cañón

car el coche; **~ hire [BE]** el alquiler de coches; **~ park [BE]** el aparcamiento; **~ rental** el alquiler de coches; **~ seat** el asiento de niño

carafe la garrafa

card la tarjeta; **ATM ~** la tarjeta de cajero automático; **credit ~** la tarjeta de crédito; **debit ~** la tarjeta de débito; **phone ~** la tarjeta telefónica

carry-on (piece of hand luggage) el equipaje de mano

cart (grocery store) el carrito; **~ (luggage)** el carrito para el equipaje

carton el cartón; **~ of cigarettes** el cartón de tabaco

case (amount) la caja

cash *v* cobrar; **~** *n* el efectivo; **~ advance** sacar dinero de la tarjeta

cashier el cajero

casino el casino

castle el castillo

cathedral la catedral

cave la cueva
CD el CD
cell phone el teléfono móvil
Celsius el grado centígrado
centimeter el centímetro
certificate el certificado
chair la silla; **~ lift** la telesilla
change v (buses) cambiar;
  ~ n (money) el cambio
charcoal el carbón
charge v (credit card) cobrar;
  ~ n (cost) el precio
cheap barato
cheaper más barato
check v (on something) revisar;
  ~ v (luggage) facturar;
  ~ n (payment) el cheque;
  ~-in (airport) la facturación;
  ~-in (hotel) el registro;
  ~ing account la cuenta corriente;
  ~-out (hotel) la salida
Cheers! ¡Salud!
chemical toilet el váter químico
chemist [BE] la farmacia
cheque [BE] el cheque
chest (body part) el pecho;
  ~ pain el dolor de pecho
chewing gum el chicle
child el niño; **~ seat** la silla
  para niños
children's menu el menú para niños

children's portion la ración
  para niños
Chinese chino
chopsticks los palillos chinos
church la iglesia
cigar el puro
cigarette el cigarrillo
class la clase; **business ~** la clase
  preferente; **economy ~** la clase
  económica; **first ~** la primera clase
classical music la música clásica
clean v limpiar; **~** adj limpio; **~ing
  product** el producto de limpieza;
  ~ing supplies los productos
  de limpieza
clear v (on an ATM) borrar
cliff el acantilado
cling film [BE] el film transparente
close v (a shop) cerrar
closed cerrado
clothing la ropa; **~ store** la tienda
  de ropa
club la discoteca
coat el abrigo
coffee shop la cafetería
coin la moneda
colander el escurridor
cold n (sickness) el catarro;
  ~ adj (temperature) frío
colleague el compañero de trabajo
cologne la colonia

color el color
comb el peine
come v venir
complaint la queja
computer el ordenador
concert el concierto; ~ **hall** la sala
de conciertos
condition (medical) el estado
de salud
conditioner el suavizante
condom el preservativo
conference la conferencia
confirm v confirmar
congestion la congestión
connect v **(internet)** conectarse
connection (internet) la conexión;
~ **(flight)** la conexión de vuelo
constipated estreñido
consulate el consulado
consultant el consultor
contact v ponerse en contacto con
contact lens la lentilla de contacto;
~ **solution** el líquido de lentillas
de contacto
contagious contagioso
convention hall el salón
de congresos
conveyor belt la cinta
transportadora
cook v cocinar
cooking gas el gas butano

cool (temperature) frío
copper el cobre
corkscrew el sacacorchos
cost v costar
cot el catre
cotton el algodón
cough v toser; ~ n la tos
country code el código de país
cover charge la entrada
crash v **(car)** estrellarse
cream (ointment) la pomada
credit card la tarjeta de crédito
crew neck el cuello redondo
crib la cuna
crystal el cristal
cup la taza
currency la moneda; ~ **exchange**
el cambio de divisas; ~ **exchange**
office la casa de cambio
current account [BE] la cuenta
corriente
customs las aduanas
cut v **(hair)** cortar; ~ n **(injury)**
el corte
cute mono
cycling el ciclismo

D

damage v causar daño
damaged ha sufrido daños
dance v bailar; ~ **club** la discoteca

dangerous peligroso
dark oscuro
date (calendar) la fecha
day el día
deaf sordo
debit card la tarjeta de débito
deck chair la tumbona
declare v declarar
decline v **(credit card)** rechazar
deeply hondo
degrees (temperature) los grados
delay v retrasarse
delete v **(computer)** borrar
delicatessen la charcutería
delicious delicioso
denim tela vaquero
dentist el dentista
denture la dentadura
deodorant el desodorante
department store los grandes
almacenes
departures (airport) las salidas
deposit v depositar; ~ n **(bank)**
el depósito bancario;
~ v **(reserve a room)** la fianza
desert el desierto
dessert el postre
detergent el detergente
develop v **(film)** revelar
diabetic diabético
dial v marcar

diamond el diamante
diaper el pañal
diarrhea la diarrea
diesel el diesel
difficult difícil
digital digital; ~ **camera**
la cámara digital; ~ **photos**
las fotos digitales; ~ **prints**
las fotos digitales
dining room el comedor
dinner la cena
direction la dirección
dirty sucio
disabled discapacitado;
~ **accessible [BE]** el acceso para
discapacitados
discharge (bodily fluid)
la secreción
disconnect (computer) desconecta
discount el descuento
dish (kitchen) el plato; ~**washer**
el lavavajillas; ~**washing liquid**
el líquido lavavajillas
display v mostrar; ~ **case** la vitrin.
disposable desechable;
~ **razor** la cuchilla desechable
dive v bucear
diving equipment el equipo
de buceo
divorce v divorciar
dizzy mareado

doctor el médico

doll la muñeca

dollar (U.S.) el dólar

domestic nacional; ~ **flight** el vuelo nacional

door la puerta

dormitory el dormitorio

double bed la cama de matrimonio

downtown el centro

dozen la docena

drag lift el telesquí

dress (piece of clothing) el vestido; ~ **code** las normas de vestuario

drink *v* beber; ~ *n* la bebida; ~ **menu** la carta de bebidas; ~**ing water** el agua potable

drive *v* conducir

driver's license number el número de permiso de conducir

drop (medicine) la gota

drowsiness la somnolencia

dry cleaner la tintorería

dubbed doblada

during durante

duty (tax) el impuesto; ~**-free** libre de impuestos

DVD el DVD

E

ear la oreja; ~**ache** el dolor de oído

earlier más temprano

early temprano

earrings los pendientes

east el este

easy fácil

eat *v* comer

economy class la clase económica

elbow el codo

electric outlet el enchufe eléctrico

elevator el ascensor

e-mail *v* enviar un correo electrónico; ~ *n* el correo electrónico; ~ **address** la dirección de correo electrónico

emergency la emergencia; ~ **exit** la salida de urgencia

empty *v* vaciar

enamel (jewelry) el esmalte

end *v* terminar

English el inglés

engrave *v* grabar

enjoy *v* disfrutar

enter *v* entrar

entertainment el entretenimiento

entrance la entrada

envelope el sobre

equipment el equipo

escalators las escaleras mecánicas

e-ticket el billete electrónico

EU resident el/la residente de la UE

euro el euro

evening la noche

excess el exceso

exchange v (money) cambiar;
~ v (goods) devolver;
~ n (place) la casa de cambio;
~ rate el tipo de cambio

excursion la excursión

excuse v (to get past) pedir perdón;
~ v (to get attention) disculparse

exhausted agotado

exit v salir; ~ n la salida

expensive caro

expert (skill level) experto

exposure (film) la foto

express rápido; ~ bus el autobús
rápido; ~ train el tren rápido

extension (phone) la extensión

extra adicional; ~ large equis
ele (XL)

extract v (tooth) extraer

eye el ojo

eyebrow wax la depilación de cejas

F

face la cara

facial la limpieza de cutis

family la familia

fan (appliance) el ventilador;
~ (souvenir) el abanico

far lejos; ~-sighted hipermétrope

farm la granja

fast rápido; ~ food la comida rápida

faster más rápido

fat free sin grasa

father el padre

fax v enviar un fax; ~ n el fax;
~ number el número de fax

fee la tasa

feed v alimentar

ferry el ferry

fever la fiebre

field (sports) el campo

fill v llenar ; ~ out v
(form) rellenar

filling (tooth) el empaste

film (camera) el carrete

fine (fee for breaking law)
la multa

finger el dedo; ~nail la uña
del dedo

fire fuego; ~ department los
bomberos; ~ door la puerta de
incendios

first primero; ~ class la primera
clase

fit (clothing) quedar bien

fitting room el probador

fix v (repair) reparar

flashlight la linterna

flight el vuelo

floor el suelo

flower la flor

folk music la música folk

food la comida
foot el pie
football [BE] el fútbol
for para/por
forecast el pronóstico
forest el bosque
fork el tenedor
form el formulario
formula (baby) la fórmula infantil
fort el fuerte
fountain la fuente
free gratuito
freezer el congelador
fresh fresco
friend el amigo
frying pan la sartén
full completo;
   ~-service el servicio completo;
   ~-time a tiempo completo

G

game el partido
garage (parking) el garaje;
   ~ (repair) el taller
garbage bag la bolsa de basura
gas la gasolina; **~ station**
   la gasolinera
gate (airport) la puerta
gay gay; **~ bar** el bar gay;
   ~ club la discoteca gay
gel (hair) la gomina

get to *v* ir a
get off *v* **(a train/bus/subway)**
   bajarse
gift el regalo; **~ shop** la tienda
   de regalos
girl la niña; **~friend** la novia
give *v* dar
glass (drinking) el vaso;
   ~ (material) el vidrio
glasses las gafas
go *v* **(somewhere)** ir a
gold el oro
golf golf; **~ course** el campo de
   golf; **~ tournament** el torneo
   de golf
good *n* el producto; **~** *adj* bueno;
   ~ afternoon buenas tardes;
   ~ evening buenas noches;
   ~ morning buenos días;
   ~bye adiós
gram el gramo
grandchild el nieto
grandparent el abuelo
gray gris
green verde
grocery store el supermercado
ground la tierra; **~ floor** la planta
   baja; **~cloth** la tela impermeable
group el grupo
guide el guía; **~ book** la guía;
   ~ dog el perro guía

gym el gimnasio
gynecologist el ginecólogo

H

hair el pelo; ~ **dryer** el secador de pelo; ~ **salon** la peluquería; ~**brush** el cepillo de pelo; ~**cut** el corte de pelo; ~**spray** la laca; ~**style** el peinado; ~**stylist** el estilista
half medio; ~ **hour** la media hora; ~-**kilo** el medio kilo
hammer el martillo
hand la mano; ~ **luggage [BE]** el equipaje de mano; ~**bag [BE]** el bolso
handicapped discapacitado; ~-**accessible** el acceso para discapacitados
hangover la resaca
happy feliz
hat el sombrero
have v tener
head (body part) la cabeza; ~**ache** el dolor de cabeza; ~**phones** los cascos
health la salud; ~ **food store** la tienda de alimentos naturales
heart el corazón; ~ **condition** padecer del corazón
heat v calentar; ~ n el calor

heater [heating BE] la calefacción
hello hola
helmet el casco
help v ayudar; ~ n la ayuda
here aquí
hi hola
high alto; ~**chair** la trona; ~**way** la autopista
hiking boots las botas de montaña
hill la colina
hire v [BE] alquilar; ~ **car [BE]** el coche de alquiler
hitchhike v hacer autostop
hockey el hockey
holiday [BE] las vacaciones
horse track el hipódromo
hospital el hospital
hostel el albergue
hot (temperature) caliente; ~ **(spicy)** picante; ~ **spring** el agua termale; ~ **water** el agua caliente
hotel el hotel
hour la hora
house la casa; ~**hold goods** los artículos para el hogar; ~**keeping services** el servicio de limpieza de habitaciones
how (question) cómo; ~ **much (question)** cuánto cuesta
hug v abrazar

hungry hambriento
hurt *v* **(have pain)** tener dolor
husband el marido

I

ibuprofen el ibuprofeno
ice el hielo; **~ hockey** el hockey sobre hielo
icy *adj* helado
identification el documento de identidad
ill *v* **(to feel)** encontrarse mal
in dentro
include *v* incluir
indoor pool la piscina cubierta
inexpensive barato
infected infectado
information (phone) el número de teléfono de información; **~ desk** el mostrador de información
insect el insecto; **~ bite** la picadura de insecto; **~ repellent** el repelente de insectos
insert *v* introducir
insomnia el insomnio
instant message el mensaje instantáneo
insulin la insulina
insurance el seguro; **~ card** la tarjeta de seguro; **~ company** la compañía de seguros

interesting interesante
intermediate el nivel intermedio
international (airport area) internacional; **~ flight** el vuelo internacional; **~ student card** la tarjeta internacional de estudiante
internet la internet; **~ cafe** el cibercafé; **~ service** el servicio de internet; **wireless ~** el acceso inalámbrico
interpreter el/la intérprete
intersection el cruce
intestine el intestino
introduce *v* presentar
invoice [BE] la factura
Ireland Irlanda
Irish irlandés
iron *v* planchar; **~** *n* **(clothes)** la plancha
Italian italiano

J

jacket la chaqueta
jar el bote
jaw la mandíbula
jazz el jazz; **~ club** el club de jazz
jeans los vaqueros
jet ski la moto acuática
jeweler la joyería
jewelry las joyas

join v acompañar a
joint (body part) la articulación

K

key la llave; **~ card** la llave electrónica; **~ ring** el llavero
kiddie pool la piscina infantil
kidney (body part) el riñón
kilo el kilo; **~gram** el kilogramo; **~meter** el kilómetro
kiss v besar
kitchen la cocina; **~ foil [BE]** el papel de aluminio
knee la rodilla
knife el cuchillo

L

lace el encaje
lactose intolerant alérgico a la lactosa
lake el lago
large grande; **~er** más grande
last último
late (time) tarde; **~er** más tarde
launderette [BE] la lavandería
laundromat la lavandería
laundry la colada; **~ facility** la lavandería; **~ service** el servicio de lavandería
lawyer el abogado
leather el cuero

to leave v salir
left (direction) la izquierda
leg la pierna
lens la lente
less menos
lesson la lección
letter la carta
library la biblioteca
life la vida; **~ jacket** el chaleco salvavidas; **~guard** el socorrista
lift n [BE] el ascensor; **~** v (to give a ride) llevar en coche; **~ pass** el pase de acceso a los remontes
light n (overhead) la luz; **~** v (cigarette) dar fuego; **~bulb** la bombilla
lighter el mechero
like v gustar; **I like** me gusta
line (train) la línea
linen el lino
lip el labio
liquor store la tienda de bebidas alcohólicas
liter el litro
little pequeño
live v vivir
liver (body part) el hígado
loafers los mocasines
local de la zona
lock v cerrar; **~** n el cerrojo
locker la taquilla

log on *v* **(computer)** iniciar sesión

log off *v* **(computer)** cerrar sesión

long largo; **~ sleeves**
las mangas largas; **~-sighted [BE]**
hipermétrope

look *v* mirar

lose *v* **(something)** perder

lost perdido; **~ and found**
la oficina de objetos perdidos

lotion la crema hidratante

louder más alto

love *v* querer; **~** *n* el amor

low bajo; **~er** más bajo

luggage el equipaje; **~ cart**
el carrito de equipaje; **~ locker**
la consigna automática; **~ ticket**
el talón de equipaje; **hand ~ [BE]**
el equipaje de mano

lunch la comida

lung el pulmón

M

magazine la revista

magnificent magnífico

mail *v* enviar por correo;
~ *n* el correo; **~box** el buzón
de correo

main principal; **~ attractions**
los principales sitios de interés;
~ course el plato principal

make up a prescription *v* **[BE]**
despachar medicamentos

mall el centro comercial

man el hombre

manager el gerente

manicure la manicura

manual car el coche con
transmisión manual

map el mapa

market el mercado

married casado

marry *v* casarse

mass (church service) la misa

massage el masaje

match la cerilla

meal la comida

measure *v* **(someone)** medir

measuring cup la taza medidora

measuring spoon la cuchara
medidora

mechanic el mecánico

medicine el medicamento

medium (size) mediano

meet *v* **(someone)** conocer

meeting la reunión; **~ room**
la sala de reuniones

membership card la tarjeta de socio

memorial (place) el monumento
conmemorativo

memory card la tarjeta de
memoria

mend *v* zurcir

menstrual cramps los dolores menstruales
menu la carta
message el mensaje
meter (parking) el parquímetro
microwave el microondas
midday [BE] el mediodía
midnight la medianoche
mileage el kilometraje
mini-bar el minibar
minute el minuto
missing desaparecido
mistake el error
mobile móvil; ~ **home** la caravana; ~ **phone** [BE] el teléfono móvil
mobility la movilidad
money el dinero
month el mes
mop la fregona
moped el ciclomotor
more más
morning la mañana
mosque la mezquita
mother la madre
motion sickness el mareo
motor el motor; ~ **boat** la lancha motora; ~**cycle** la motocicleta; ~**way** [BE] la autopista
mountain la montaña; ~ **bike** la bicicleta de montaña

mousse (hair) la espuma para el pelo
mouth n la boca
movie la película; ~ **theater** el cine
mug v asaltar
muscle (body part) el músculo
museum el museo
music la música; ~ **store** la tienda de música

N

nail la uña; ~ **file** la lima de uñas; ~ **salon** el salon de manicura
name el nombre
napkin la servilleta
nappy [BE] el pañale
nationality la nacionalidad
nature preserve la reserva natural
(be) nauseous v tener náuseas
near cerca; ~**-sighted** miope; ~**by** cerca de aquí
neck el cuello
necklace el collar
need v necesitar
newspaper el periódico
newsstand el quiosco
next próximo
nice adj amable
night la noche; ~**club** la discoteca

no no

non sin; **~-alcoholic** sin alcohol;
  ~-smoking para no fumadores

noon el mediodía

north el norte

nose la nariz

note [BE] el billete

nothing nada

notify v avisar

novice (skill level) principiante

now ahora

number el número

nurse el enfermero/la enfermera

O

office la oficina; **~ hours
(doctor's)** las horas de consulta; **~
hours (other offices)** el horario
de oficina

off-licence [BE] la tienda de
bebidas alcohólicas

oil el aceite

OK de acuerdo

old adj viejo

on the corner en la esquina

once una vez

one uno; **~-way ticket** el billete
de ida; **~-way street** la calle de
sentido único

only solamente

open v abrir; **~** adj abierto

opera la ópera; **~ house** el teatro
de la ópera

opposite frente a

optician el oculista

orange (color) naranja

orchestra la orquesta

order v pedir

outdoor pool la piscina exterior

outside fuera

over sobre; **~ the counter
(medication)** sin receta; **~look
(scenic place)** el mirador;
  ~night por la noche

oxygen treatment
la oxígenoterapia

P

p.m. de la tarde

pacifier el chupete

pack v hacer las maletas

package el paquete

paddling pool [BE] la piscina
infantil

pad [BE] la compresa

pain el dolor

pajamas los pijamas

palace el palacio

pants los pantalones

pantyhose las medias

paper el papel; **~ towel** el papel
de cocina

paracetamol [BE] el paracetamol
park v aparcar; ~ n el parque;
  ~ing garage el párking;
  ~ing lot el aparcamiento
parliament building el palacio de
  las cortes
part (for car) la pieza; **~-time**
  a tiempo parcial
pass through v estar de paso
passenger el pasajero
passport el pasaporte; **~ control**
  el control de pasaportes
password la contraseña
pastry shop la pastelería
path el camino
pay v pagar; **~ phone** el teléfono
  público
peak (of a mountain) la cima
pearl la perla
pedestrian el peatón
pediatrician el pediatra
pedicure la pedicura
pen el bolígrafo
penicillin la penicilina
penis el pene
per por; **~ day** por día;
  ~ hour por hora; **~ night** por
  noche; **~ week** por semana
perfume el perfume
period (menstrual) la regla;
  ~ (of time) la época

permit v permitir
petite las tallas pequeñas
petrol la gasolina; **~ station**
  la gasolinera
pewter el peltre
pharmacy la farmacia
phone v hacer una llamada;
  ~ n el teléfono; **~ call** la llamada
  de teléfono; **~ card** la tarjeta
  telefónica; **~ number** el número
  de teléfono
photo la foto; **~copy** la fotocopia;
  ~graphy la fotografía
pick up v (something) recoger
picnic area la zona para picnic
piece el trozo
Pill (birth control) la píldora
pillow la almohada
**personal identification number
  (PIN)** la clave
pink rosa
piste [BE] la pista; **~ map
  [BE]** el mapa de pistas
pizzeria la pizzería
place v (a bet) hacer una apuesta
plane el avión
plastic wrap el film transparente
plate el plato
platform [BE] (train) el andén
platinum el platino
play v jugar; **~** n (theater) la obra

de teatro; **~ground** el patio de
recreo; **~pen** el parque
please por favor
pleasure el placer
plunger el desatascador
plus size la talla grande
pocket el bolsillo
poison el veneno
poles (skiing) los bastones
police la policía; **~ report**
el certificado de la policía;
~ station la comisaría
pond el estanque
pool la piscina
pop music la música pop
portion la ración
post [BE] el correo;
~ office la oficina de correos;
~box [BE] el buzón de correos;
~card la tarjeta postal
pot la olla
pottery la cerámica
pounds (British sterling) las libras
esterlinas
pregnant embarazada
prescribe v recetar
prescription la receta
press v **(clothing)** planchar
price el precio
print v imprimir
problem el problema

produce las frutas y verduras;
~ store la frutería y verdulería
prohibit v prohibir
pronounce v pronunciar
public el público
pull v **(door sign)** tirar
purple morado
purse el bolso
push v **(door sign)** empujar;
~chair [BE] el cochecito de niño

Q

quality n la calidad
question la pregunta
quiet adj tranquilo

R

racetrack el circuito de carreras
racket (sports) la raqueta
railway station [BE] la estación
de trenes
rain la lluvia; **~coat** el
chubasquero; **~forest** el bosque
pluvial; **~y** adv lluvioso
rap (music) el rap
rape v violar; **~** n la violación
rash la erupción cutánea
razor blade la hoja de afeitar
reach v localizar
ready listo
real auténtico

receipt el recibo
receive v recibir
reception la recepción
recharge v recargar
recommend v recomendar
recommendation la recomendación
recycle v reciclar
red rojo
refrigerator n la nevera
region la región
registered mail el correo certificado
regular normal
relationship la relación
rent v alquilar
rental car el coche de alquiler
repair v arreglar
repeat v repetir
reservation la reserva;
~ **desk** la taquilla
reserve v reservar
restaurant el restaurante
restroom el servicio
retired jubilado
return v **(something)** devolver;
~ n **[BE]** la ida y vuelta
rib (body part) la costilla
right (direction) derecha;
~ **of way** prioridad de paso
ring el anillo
river n el río
road map el mapa de carreteras

rob v atracar
robbed atracado
romantic romántico
room la habitación; ~ **key** la
llave de habitación; ~ **service** el
servicio de habitaciones
round-trip ida y vuelta
route la ruta
rowboat la barca de remos
rubbish [BE] la basura; ~ **bag [BE]**
la bolsa de basura
rugby el rubgy
ruins las ruinas
rush la prisa

S

sad triste
safe n la caja fuerte; ~ adj seguro
sales tax el IVA
same mismo
sandals las sandalias
sanitary napkin la compresa
saucepan el cazo
sauna la sauna
save v **(computer)** guardar
savings (account) la cuenta
de ahorro
scanner el escáner
scarf la bufanda
schedule v programar;
~ n el horario

school el colegio
science la ciencia
scissors las tijeras
sea el mar
seat el asiento
security la seguridad
see v ver
self-service el autoservicio
sell v vender
seminar el seminario
send v enviar
senior citizen jubilado
separated (marriage) -separado
serious serio
service (in a restaurant) el servicio
sexually transmitted disease (STD) la enfermedad de transmisión sexual
shampoo el champú
sharp afilado
shaving cream la crema de afeitar
sheet la sábana
ship v enviar
shirt la camisa
shoe store la zapatería
shoes los zapatos
shop v comprar
shopping ir de compras;
~ **area** la zona de compras;
~ **centre [BE]** el centro comercial;
~ **mall** el centro comercial
short corto; ~ **sleeves** las mangas
cortas; ~**s** los pantalones cortos;
~-**sighted [BE]** miope
shoulder el hombro
show v enseñar
shower la ducha
shrine el santuario
sick enfermo
side el lado; ~ **dish** la guarnición;
~ **effect** el efecto secundario;
~ **order** la guarnición
sightsee v hacer turismo
sightseeing tour el recorrido
turístico
sign v **(name)** firmar
silk la seda
silver la plata
single (unmarried) soltero; ~ **bed**
la cama; ~ **prints** una copia;
~ **room** una habitación individual
sink el lavabo
sister la hermana
sit v sentarse
size la talla
skin la piel
skirt la falda
ski v esquiar; ~ n el esquí; ~ **lift**
el telesquí
sleep v dormir; ~**er car** el coche
cama; ~**ing bag** el saco de dormir
slice v cortar en rodajas
slippers las zapatillas

slower más despacio
slowly despacio
small pequeño
smaller más pequeño
smoke v fumar
smoking (area) la zona de fumadores
snack bar la cafetería
sneakers las zapatillas de deporte
snorkeling equipment el equipo de esnórquel
snow la nieve; ~**board** la tabla de snowboard; ~**shoe** la raqueta de nieve; ~**y** nevado
soap el jabón
soccer el fútbol
sock el calcetín
some alguno
soother [BE] el chupete
sore throat las anginas
sorry lo siento
south el sur
souvenir el recuerdo; ~ **store** la tienda de recuerdos
spa el centro de salud y belleza
Spain España
Spanish el español
spatula la espátula
speak v hablar
special (food) la especialidad de la casa

specialist (doctor) el especialista
specimen el ejemplar
speeding el exceso de velocidad
spell v deletrear
spicy picante
spine (body part) la columna vertebral
spoon la cuchara
sports los deportes; ~ **massage** el masaje deportivo
sporting goods store la tienda de deportes
sprain el esguince
square cuadrado; ~ **kilometer** el kilómetro cuadrado; ~ **meter** el metro cuadrado
stadium el estadio
stairs las escaleras
stamp v **(a ticket)** picar; ~ n **(postage)** el sello
start v empezar
starter [BE] el aperitivo
station la estación; **bus ~** la estación de autobuses; **gas ~** la gasolinera; **muster ~ [BE]** el punto de reunión; **petrol ~ [BE]** la gasolinera; **subway ~** el metro; **train ~** la estación de tren
statue la estatua
stay v quedarse
steal v robar

steep empinado

sterling silver la plata esterlina

sting el escozor

stolen robado

stomach el estómago; **~ache**
el dolor de estómago

stop v pararse; **~** n la parada

storey [BE] la planta

stove el horno

straight recto

strange extraño

stream el arroyo

stroller el cochecito

student el estudiante

study v estudiar

stunning impresionante

subtitle el subtítulo

subway el metro; **~ station**
la estación de metro

suit el traje

suitcase la maleta

sun el sol; **~block** el protector
solar total; **~burn** la quemadura
solar; **~glasses** las gafas
de sol; **~ny** soleado; **~screen**
el protector solar; **~stroke**
la insolación

super (fuel) súper; **~market**
el supermercado

surfboard la tabla de surf

surgical spirit [BE] el alcohol

etílico

swallow v tragar

sweater el jersey

sweatshirt la sudadera

sweet (taste) dulce; **~s [BE]**
los caramelos

swelling la hinchazón

swim v nadar; **~suit** el bañador

symbol (keyboard) el símbolo

synagogue la sinagoga

T

table la mesa

tablet (medicine) el comprimido

take v llevar; **~ away [BE]**
para llevar

tampon el tampón

tapas bar el bar de tapas

taste v probar

taxi el taxi

team el equipo

telephone el teléfono

temporary provisional

tennis el tenis

tent la tienda de campaña;
~ peg la estaca; **~ pole** el mástil

terminal (airport) la terminal

terracotta la terracotta

terrible terrible

text v (send a message) enviar
un mensaje de texto;

~ *n* (**message**) el texto
thank *v* dar las gracias a;
~ **you** gracias
that eso
theater el teatro
there ahí
thief el ladrón
thigh el muslo
thirsty sediento
this esto
throat la garganta
ticket el billete; ~ **office**
el despacho de billetes; ~**ed**
passenger el pasajero con billete
tie (**clothing**) la corbata
time el tiempo; ~**table** [BE]
el horario
tire la rueda
tired cansado
tissue el pañuelo de paper
tobacconist el estanco
today hoy
toe el dedo del pie; ~**nail** la uña
del pie
toilet [BE] el servicio; ~ **paper**
el papel higiénico
tomorrow mañana
tongue la lengua
tonight esta noche
too demasiado
tooth el diente; ~**brush** el cepillo

de dientes; ~**paste** la pasta de
dientes
total (**amount**) el total
tough (**food**) duro
tourist el turista; ~ **information**
office la oficina de turismo
tour el recorrido turístico
tow truck la grúa
towel la toalla
tower la torre
town la ciudad; ~ **hall**
el ayuntamiento; ~ **map** el mapa
de ciudad; ~ **square** la plaza
toy el juguete; ~ **store** la tienda
de juguetes
track (**train**) el andén
traditional tradicional
traffic light el semáforo
trail la pista; ~ **map** el mapa de
la pista
trailer el remolque
train el tren; ~ **station** la estación
de tren
transfer *v* cambiar
translate *v* traducir
trash la basura
travel *v* viajar; ~ **agency**
la agencia de viajes; ~ **sickness**
el mareo; ~**er's check**
[**cheque** BE] el cheque de viaje
tree el árbol

trim (hair cut) cortarse las puntas
trip el viaje
trolley [BE] el carrito
trousers [BE] los pantalones
T-shirt la camiseta
turn off v apagar
turn on v encender
TV la televisión
type v escribir a máquina
tyre [BE] la rueda

U

United Kingdom (U.K.) el Reino Unido
United States (U.S.) los Estados Unidos
ugly feo
umbrella el paraguas
unattended desatendido
unconscious inconsciente
underground [BE] el metro; ~ **station [BE]** la estación de metro
underpants [BE] los calzoncillos
understand v entender
underwear la ropa interior
university la universidad
unleaded (gas) la gasolina sin plomo
upper superior
urgent urgente
use v usar

username el nombre de usuario
utensil el cubierto

V

vacancy la habitación libre
vacation las vacaciones
vaccination la vacuna
vacuum cleaner la aspiradora
vaginal infection la infección vaginal
valid validez
valley el valle
valuable valioso
VAT [BE] el IVA
vegetarian vegetariano
vehicle registration el registro del coche
viewpoint [BE] el mirador
village el pueblo
vineyard la viña
visa (passport document) el visado
visit v visitar; ~**ing hours** el horario de visita
visually impaired la persona con discapacidad visual
vitamin la vitamina
V-neck el cuello de pico
vomit v vomitar

W

wait v esperar; ~ n la espera;
~**ing room** la sala de espera
waiter el camarero
waitress la camarera
wake v despertarse; ~**-up call**
la llamada despertador
walk v caminar; ~ n la caminata;
~**ing route** la ruta de senderismo
wallet la cartera
warm v (**something**) calentar;
~ adj (**temperature**) calor
washing machine la lavadora
watch el reloj
waterfall la cascada
weather el tiempo
week la semana; ~**end** el fin de
semana; ~**ly** semanal
welcome v acoger
well bien; ~**-rested** descansado
west el oeste
what (**question**) qué
wheelchair la silla de ruedas;
~ **ramp** la rampa para silla
de ruedas
when (**question**) cuándo
where (**question**) dónde
white blanco; ~ **gold** el oro blanco
who (**question**) quién
widowed viudo
wife la mujer

window la ventana; ~ **case**
el escaparate
windsurfer el surfista
wine list la carta de vinos
wireless inalámbrico; ~ **internet**
el acceso inalámbrico a internet;
~ **internet service** el servicio
inalámbrico a internet; ~ **phone**
el teléfono móvil
with con
withdraw v retirar;
~**al** (**bank**) retirar fondos
without sin
woman la mujer
wool la lana
work v trabajar
wrap v envolver
wrist la muñeca
write v escribir

Y

year el año
yellow amarillo
yes sí
yesterday ayer
young joven
youth hostel el albergue
juvenil

Z

zoo el zoológico

A

a tiempo completo full-time
a tiempo parcial part-time
la abadía abbey
el abanico fan (souvenir)
abierto *adj* open
el abogado lawyer
abrazar *v* hug
el abrebotellas bottle opener
el abrelatas can opener
el abrigo coat
abrir *v* open
el abuelo grandparent
aburrido boring
acampar *v* camp
el acantilado cliff
el acceso access;
  ~ inalámbrico a internet
  wireless internet; **~ para
  discapacitados** handicapped-
  [disabled- BE] accessible
el accidente accident
el aceite oil
aceptar *v* accept
acoger *v* welcome
acompañar a *v* join
la acupuntura acupuncture
el adaptador adapter
adicional extra

adiós goodbye
las aduanas customs
el aeropuerto airport
afilado sharp
la agencia agency; **~ de
  viajes** travel agency
agotado exhausted
el agua water; **~ caliente**
  hot water; **~ potable** drinking
  water
las aguas termales hot spring
ahí there
ahora now
el aire air, air pump;
  ~ acondicionado air conditioning
el albergue hostel;
  ~ juvenil youth hostel
alérgico allergic;
  ~ a la lactosa lactose intolerant
algo anything
el algodón cotton
alguno some
alimentar *v* feed
el allanamiento de morada
  break-in (burglary)
la almohada pillow
el alojamiento accommodation
alquilar *v* rent [hire BE];
  el ~ de coches car rental [hire BE]

alto high
amable nice
amarillo yellow
la ambulancia ambulance
el amigo friend
el amor n love
el andén track [platform BE] (train)
anémico anemic
la anestesia anesthesia
las anginas sore throat
el anillo ring
el animal animal
antes de before
el antibiótico antibiotic
el año year
apagar v turn off
el aparcamiento parking lot
   [car park BE]
aparcar v park
el apartamento apartment
el apéndice appendix (body part)
el aperitivo appetizer [starter BE]
aquí here
el árbol tree
la aromaterapia aromatherapy
arreglar v repair
el arroyo stream
la arteria artery
la articulación joint (body part)
los artículos goods; **~ para el**
   hogar household good

la artritis arthritis
asaltar v mug
el asalto attack
el ascensor elevator [lift BE]
asiático Asian
el asiento seat; **~ de niño** car
   seat; **~ de pasillo** aisle seat
asistir v attend
asmático asthmatic
la aspiradora vacuum cleaner
la aspirina aspirin
atracado robbed
atracar v rob
Australia Australia
australiano Australian
auténtico real
el autobús bus; **~ rápido**
   express bus
automático automatic
la autopista highway
   [motorway BE]
el autoservicio self-service
la avería breakdown
el avión airplane, plane
avisar v notify
ayer yesterday
la ayuda n help
ayudar v help
el ayuntamiento town hall
azul blue

B

bailar v dance
bajarse v get off (a train, bus, subway)
bajo low
el ballet ballet
el baloncesto basketball
el bálsamo para después del afeitado aftershave
el banco bank
el bañador swimsuit
el baño bathroom
el bar bar; ~ **de tapas** tapas bar; ~ **gay** gay bar
barato cheap, inexpensive
la barbacoa barbecue
la barca de remos rowboat
el barco boat
los bastones poles (skiing)
la basura trash [rubbish BE]
la batería battery (car)
el bebé baby
beber v drink
la bebida n drink
beis beige
el béisbol baseball
besar v kiss
el biberón baby bottle
la biblioteca library
la bicicleta bicycle; ~ **de montaña** mountain bike

el billete n bill (money); ~ ticket; ~ **de autobús** bus ticket; ~ **de ida** one-way (ticket); ~ **de ida y vuelta** round trip [return BE]; ~ **electrónico** e-ticket
el biquini bikini
blanco white
la blusa blouse
la boca mouth
el bolígrafo pen
la bolsa de basura garbage [rubbish BE] bag
el bolsillo pocket
el bolso purse [handbag BE]
los bomberos fire department
la bombilla lightbulb
borrar v clear (on an ATM); ~ v delete (computer)
el bosque forest; ~ **pluvial** rainforest
las botas boots; ~ **de montaña** hiking boots
el bote jar
la botella bottle
el brazo arm
británico British
el broche brooch
bucear to dive
bueno adj good
buenas noches good evening
buenas tardes good afternoon

buenos días good morning
la bufanda scarf
el buzón de correo mailbox
  [postbox BE]

C

la cabaña cabin (house)
el cabaré cabaret
la cabeza head (body part)
la cafetería cafe, coffee shop, snack
  bar
la caja case (amount);
  ~ fuerte n safe
el cajero cashier;
  ~ automático ATM
el calcetín sock
la calefacción heater [heating BE]
calentar v heat, warm
la calidad quality
la calle de sentido único one-way
  street
calor hot, warm (temperature)
las calorías calories
los calzoncillos briefs [underpants
  BE] (clothing)
la cama single bed; **~ de
  matrimonio** double bed
la cámara camera;
  ~ digital digital camera
la camarera waitress
el camarero waiter

el camarote cabin (ship)
cambiar v change, exchange, transfer
el cambio n change (money);
  ~ de divisas currency exchange
caminar v walk
la caminata n walk
el camino path
la camisa shirt
la camiseta T-shirt
el cámping campsite
el campo field (sports);
  ~ de batalla battleground;
  ~ de golf golf course
Canadá Canada
canadiense Canadian
cancelar v cancel
el/la canguro babysitter
cansado tired
el cañón canyon
la cara face
los caramelos candy [sweets BE]
la caravana mobile home
el carbón charcoal
el carnicero butcher
caro expensive
el carrete film (camera)
el carrito cart [trolley BE] (grocery
  store); **~ de equipaje** luggage cart
la carta letter
la carta n menu; **~ de
  bebidas** drink menu; **~ para**

niños children's menu; **~ de vinos** wine list

la cartera *n* wallet

el cartón carton; **~ de tabaco** carton of cigarettes

la casa house; **~ de cambio** currency exchange office

casado married

casarse *v* marry

la cascada waterfall

el casco helmet

los cascos headphones

el casino casino

el castillo castle

el catarro cold (sickness)

la catedral cathedral

el catre cot

causar daño *v* damage

el cazo saucepan

el CD CD

la cena dinner

el centímetro centimeter

el centro downtown area; **~ comercial** shopping mall [centre BE]; **~ de negocios** business center; **~ de salud y belleza** spa

el cepillo de pelo hair brush

la cerámica pottery

cerca near; **~ de aquí** nearby

la cerilla *n* match

cerrado closed

cerrar *v* close, lock; **~ sesión** *v* log off (computer)

el cerrojo *n* lock

el certificado certificate; **~ de la policía** police report

la cesta basket (grocery store)

el chaleco salvavidas life jacket

el champú shampoo

la chaqueta jacket

la charcutería delicatessen

el cheque *n* check [cheque BE] (payment); **~ de viaje** traveler's check [cheque BE]

el chicle chewing gum

chino Chinese

el chubasquero raincoat

el chupete pacifier [soother BE]

el cibercafé internet cafe

el ciclismo cycling

el ciclomotor moped

la ciencia science

el cigarrillo cigarette

la cima peak (of a mountain)

el cine movie theater

la cinta transportadora conveyor belt

el cinturón *n* belt

el circuito de carreras racetrack

la cita appointment

la ciudad town

la clase class; **~ económica** economy class; **~ preferente** business class

la clave personal identification number (PIN)

el club de jazz jazz club

cobrar v bill (charge); **~** v cash; **~** v charge (credit card)

el cobre copper

el coche n car; **~ de alquiler** rental [hire BE] car; **~ automático** automatic car; **~ cama** sleeper [sleeping BE] car; **~ con transmisión manual** manual car

el cochecito stroller [pushchair BE]

la cocina kitchen

cocinar v cook

el código de país country code

el codo elbow

la colada laundry

el colegio school

la colina hill

el collar necklace

la colonia cologne

el color color

la columna vertebral spine (body part)

el comedor dining room

comer v eat

la comida food, lunch, meal;

~ rápida fast food

la comisaría police station

cómo how

el compañero de trabajo colleague

la compañia company; **~ aérea** airline; **~ de seguros** insurance company

comprar v buy, shop

la compresa sanitary napkin [pad BE]

el comprimido tablet (medicine)

con with; **~ plomo** leaded (gas)

el concierto concert

conducir v drive

conectarse v connect (internet)

la conexión connection (internet); **~ de vuelo** connection (flight)

la conferencia conference

confirmar v confirm

el congelador freezer

la congestión congestion

conocer v meet (someone)

la consigna automática luggage locker

el consulado Consulate

el consultor consultant

contagioso contagious

la contraseña password

el control de pasaportes passport control

el corazón heart

la corbata tie (clothing)

el correo *n* mail [post BE]; **~ aéreo** airmail; **~ certificado** registered mail; **~ electrónico** *n* e-mail

cortar *v* cut (hair); **~ en rodajas** to slice

cortarse las puntas *v* trim (hair cut)

el corte *n* cut (injury); **~ de pelo** haircut

corto short

costar *v* cost

la costilla rib (body part)

la crema cream; **~ antiséptica** antiseptic cream; **~ de afeitar** shaving cream; **~ hidratante** lotion

el cristal crystal

el cruce intersection

cuándo when (question)

cuánto cuesta how much

el cubierto utensil

la cuchara spoon; **~ medidora** measuring spoon

la cucharadita teaspoon

la cuchilla desechable disposable razor

el cuchillo knife

el cuello neck; **~ de pico** V-neck; **~ redondo** crew neck

el cuenco bowl

la cuenta account; **~ de ahorro** savings account; **~ corriente** checking [current BE] account

cuero leather

la cueva cave

el cumpleaños birthday

la cuna crib

D

dar to give; **~ el pecho** breastfeed; **~ fuego** light (cigarette); **~ las gracias a** *v* thank

de from, of; **~ acuerdo** OK; **~ la mañana** a.m.; **~ la tarde** p.m.; **~ la zona** local

declarar *v* declare

el dedo finger; **~ del pie** toe

deletrear *v* spell

delicioso delicious

la dentadura denture

el dentista dentist

dentro in

la depilacion wax; **~ de cejas** eyebrow wax; **~ de las ingles** bikini wax

deportes sports

depositar *v* deposit

el depósito bancario deposit (bank)

la derecha right (direction)

desaparecido missing

el desatascador plunger

desatendido unattended

el desayuno breakfast
descansado well-rested
desconectar v disconnect (computer)
el descuento discount
desechable disposable
el desierto desert
el desodorante deodorant
despachar medicamentos v fill [make up BE] a prescription
el despacho de billetes ticket office
despacio slowly
despertarse v wake
después after
el detergente detergent
detrás de behind (direction)
devolver v exchange, return (goods)
el día day
diabético diabetic
el diamante diamond
la diarrea diarrhea
el diente tooth
el diesel diesel
difícil difficult
digital digital
el dinero money
la dirección direction
la dirección address; ~ **de correo electrónico** e-mail address

discapacitado handicapped [disabled BE]
la discoteca club (dance, night); ~ **gay** gay club
disculparse v excuse (to get attention)
disfrutar v enjoy
disponible available
divorciar v divorce
doblada dubbed
doblando (la esquina) around (the corner)
la docena dozen
el documento de identidad identification
el dólar dollar (U.S.)
el dolor pain; ~ **de cabeza** headache; ~ **de espalda** backache; ~ **de estómago** stomachache; ~ **de oído** earache; ~ **de pecho** chest pain
los dolores menstruales menstrual cramps
dónde where (question)
dormir v sleep
el dormitorio dormitory
la ducha shower
dulce sweet (taste)
durante during
el DVD DVD

E

la edad age
el edificio building
el efectivo cash
el efecto secundario side effect
el ejemplar specimen
embarazada pregnant
embarcar v board
la emergencia emergency
el empaste filling (tooth)
empezar v begin, start
empinado steep
empujar v push (door sign)
en la esquina on the corner
el encaje lace
encender v turn on
el enchufe eléctrico electric outlet
encontrarse mal v be ill
la enfermedad de transmisión sexual sexually transmitted disease (STD)
el enfermero/la enfermera nurse
enfermo sick
enseñar v show
entender v understand
la entrada admission/cover charge; ~ entrance
entrar v enter
el entretenimiento entertainment
enviar v send, ship; ~ **por correo** v mail; ~ **un correo electrónico** v e-mail; ~ **un fax** v fax ; ~ **un mensaje de texto** v text (send a message)
envolver v wrap
la época period (of time)
el equipaje luggage [baggage BE]; ~ **de mano** carry-on (piece of hand luggage)
el equipo team
el equipo equipment; ~ **de buceo** diving equipment; ~ **de esnórquel** snorkeling equipment
equis ele (XL) extra large
el error mistake
la erupción cutánea rash
las escaleras stairs; ~ **mecánicas** escalators
el escáner scanner
el escaparate window case
la escoba broom
el escozor sting
escribir v write; ~ **a máquina** v type
el escurridor colander
el esguince sprain
el esmalte enamel (jewelry)
eso that
la espalda back
España Spain
el español Spanish
la espátula spatula

la especialidad de la casa special (food)

el especialista specialist (doctor)

la espera *n* wait

esperar *v* wait

la espuma para el pelo mousse (hair)

el esquí *n* ski

esquiar *v* ski

los esquís acuáticos water skis

esta noche tonight

la estaca tent peg

la estación station; ~ **de autobuses** bus station; ~ **de metro** subway [underground BE] station; ~ **de tren** train [railway BE] station

el estadio stadium

el estado de salud condition (medical)

los Estados Unidos United States (U.S.)

estadounidense American

el estanco tobacconist

el estanque pond

estar *v* be; ~ **de paso** *v* pass through

la estatua statue

el este east

el estilista hairstylist

esto this

el estómago stomach

estrellarse *v* crash (car)

estreñido constipated

estudiando studying

el estudiante student

estudiar *v* study

el euro euro

el exceso excess; ~ **de velocidad** speeding

la excursión excursion

experto expert (skill level)

la extensión extension (phone)

extraer *v* extract (tooth)

extraño strange

F

fácil *adj* easy

la factura bill [invoice BE]

la facturación check-in (airport)

facturar check (luggage)

la falda skirt

la familia family

la farmacia pharmacy [chemist BE]

el fax *n* fax

la fecha date (calendar)

feliz *adj* happy

feo *adj* ugly

el ferry ferry

la fianza deposit (to reserve a room)

la fiebre fever

el film transparente plastic wrap
  [cling film BE]
el fin de semana weekend
firmar v sign (name)
la flor flower
la fórmula infantil formula (baby)
el formulario form
la foto exposure (film);
  ~ photo; **~copia** photocopy;
  ~grafía photography;
  ~ digital digital photo
la fregona mop
los frenos brakes (car)
frente a opposite
fresco fresh
frío *adj* cold (temperature)
las frutas y verduras produce
la frutería y verdulería
  produce store
el fuego fire
la fuente fountain
fuera outside
el fuerte fort
fumar v smoke
la funda para la cámara
  camera case
el fútbol soccer [football BE]

G

las gafas glasses;
  ~ de sol sunglasses

el garaje garage (parking)
la garganta throat
la garrafa carafe
el gas butano cooking gas
la gasolina gas [petrol BE];
  ~ sin plomo unleaded gas
la gasolinera gas [petrol BE]
  station
gay gay
el gerente manager
el gimnasio gym
el ginecólogo gynecologist
la gomina gel (hair)
la gota drop (medicine)
grabar v burn (CD); ~ v engrave
gracias thank you
los grados degrees (temperature);
  ~ centígrado Celsius
el gramo gram
grande large
los grandes almacenes
  department store
la granja farm
gratuito free
gris gray
la grúa tow truck
el grupo group
guapo attractive
guardar v save (computer)
la guarnición side dish, order
el guía guide

la guía guide book; **~ de tiendas** store directory
gustar v like; **me gusta** I like

H

ha sufrido daños damaged
la habitación room;
  ~ individual single room;
  ~ libre vacancy
hablar v speak
hacer v have; **~ una apuesta**
  v place (a bet); **~ un arreglo**
  v alter; **~ una llamada** v phone;
  ~ las maletas v pack;
  ~ turismo sightseeing
hambriento hungry
helado icy
la hermana sister
el hermano brother
el hielo ice
el hígado liver (body part)
la hinchazón swelling
hipermétrope far-sighted [long-sighted BE]
el hipódromo horsetrack
el hockey hockey; **~ sobre**
  hielo ice hockey
la hoja de afeitar razor blade
hola hello
el hombre man
el hombro shoulder

hondo deeply
la hora hour
el horario n schedule [timetable BE]
los horarios hours; **~ de**
  atención al público business
  hours; **~ de oficina** office hours;
  ~ de visita visiting hours
las horas de consulta office hours
  (doctor's)
el hornillo camp stove
el horno stove
el hospital hospital
el hotel hotel
hoy today
el hueso bone

I

el ibuprofeno ibuprofen
la ida y vuelta round-trip
  [return BE]
la iglesia church
impresionante stunning
imprimir v print
el impuesto duty (tax)
incluir v include
inconsciente unconscious
increíble amazing
la infección vaginal vaginal
  infection
infectado infected
el inglés English

iniciar sesión v log on (computer)
el insecto bug
la insolación sunstroke
el insomnio insomnia
la insulina insulin
interesante interesting
internacional international
   (airport area)
la internet internet
el/la intérprete interpreter
el intestino intestine
introducir v insert
ir a v go (somewhere)
ir de compras v go shopping
Irlanda Ireland
irlandés Irish
el IVA sales tax [VAT BE]
la izquierda left (direction)

J

el jabón soap
el jardín botánico
   botanical garden
el jazz jazz
el jersey sweater
joven young
las joyas jewelry
la joyería jeweler
jubilado retired
jugar v play
el juguete toy

K

el kilo kilo; **~gramo** kilogram;
   ~metraje mileage
el kilómetro kilometer;
   ~ cuadrado square kilometer

L

el labio lip
la laca hairspray
el ladrón thief
el lago lake
la lana wool
la lancha motora motor boat
largo long
el lavabo sink
la lavadora washing machine
la lavandería laundromat
   [launderette BE]
lavar v wash
el lavavajillas dishwasher
la lección lesson
lejos far
la lengua tongue
la lente lens
las lentillas de contacto
   contact lens
las letras arts
las libras esterlinas pounds
   (British sterling)
libre de impuestos duty-free
la librería bookstore

el libro book
la lima de uñas nail file
limpiar v clean
la limpieza de cutis facial
limpio adj clean
la línea line (train)
el lino linen
la linterna flashlight
el líquido liquid; ~ **de lentillas de contacto** contact lens solution; ~ **lavavajillas** dishwashing liquid
listo ready
la litera berth
el litro liter
la llamada n call; ~ **de teléfono** phone call; ~ **despertador** wake-up call
llamar v call
la llave key; ~ **de habitación** room key; ~ **electrónica** key card
el llavero key ring
las llegadas arrivals (airport)
llegar v arrive
llenar v fill
llevar v take; ~ **en coche** lift (to give a ride)
la lluvia rain
lluvioso rainy
lo siento sorry
localizar v reach
la luz light (overhead)

M

la madre mother
magnífico magnificent
el malestar estomacal upset stomach
la maleta bag, suitcase
la mandíbula jaw
las mangas cortas short sleeves
las mangas largas long sleeves
la manicura manicure
la mano hand
la manta blanket
mañana tomorrow; **la** ~ morning
el mapa map; ~ **de carreteras** road map; ~ **de ciudad** town map; ~ **de la pista** trail [piste BE] map
el mar sea
marcar v dial
mareado dizzy
el mareo motion [travel BE] sickness
el marido husband
marrón brown
el martillo hammer
más more; ~ **alto** louder; ~ **bajo** lower; ~ **barato** cheaper; ~ **despacio** slower; ~ **grande** larger; ~ **pequeño** smaller; ~ **rápido** faster; ~ **tarde** later; ~ **temprano** earlier

el masaje massage;
  ~ deportivo sports massage
el mástil tent pole
el mecánico mechanic
el mechero lighter
la media hora half hour
mediano medium (size)
la medianoche midnight
el medicamento medicine
el médico doctor
medio half; **~ kilo** half-kilo;
  ~día noon [midday BE]
medir v measure (someone)
mejor best
menos less
el mensaje message;
  ~ instantáneo instant message
el mercado market
el mes month
la mesa table
el metro subway [underground BE]
el metro cuadrado square meter
la mezquita mosque
el microondas microwave
el minibar mini-bar
el minuto minute
el mirador overlook [viewpoint BE]
  (scenic place)
mirar v look
la misa mass (church service)
mismo same

los mocasines loafers
la mochila backpack
molestar v bother
la moneda coin, currency
mono cute
la montaña n mountain
el monumento conmemorativo
  memorial (place)
morado purple
el mostrador de información
  information desk
mostrar v display
la moto acuática jet ski
la motocicleta motorcycle
movilidad mobility
la mujer wife, woman
la multa fine (fee for breaking law)
la muñeca doll; **~** wrist
el músculo muscle
el museo museum
la música music; **~ clásica**
  classical music; **~ folk** folk music;
  ~ pop pop music
el muslo thigh

N

nacional domestic
la nacionalidad nationality
nada nothing
nadar v swim
las nalgas buttocks

naranja orange (color)
la nariz nose
necesitar v need
los negocios business
negro black
nevado snowy
la nevera refrigerator
el nieto grandchild
la niña girl
el niño boy, child
el nivel intermedio intermediate
no no
la noche evening, night
el nombre name;
  ~ de usuario username
normal regular
las normas de vestuario
  dress code
el norte north
la novia girlfriend
el novio boyfriend
el número number; **~ de fax**
  fax number; **~ de permiso**
  de conducir driver's license
  number; **~ de teléfono** phone
  number; **~ de teléfono de**
  información information (phone)

O

la obra de teatro n play (theater)
el oculista optician

el oeste west
la oficina office; **~ de correos**
  post office; **~ de objetos**
  perdidos lost and found; **~ de**
  turismo tourist information office
el ojo eye
la olla pot
la ópera opera
el ordenador computer
la oreja ear
la orina urine
el oro gold; **~ amarillo** yellow
  gold; **~ blanco** white gold
la orquesta orchestra
oscuro dark
el otro camino alternate route
la oxígenoterapia oxygen
  treatment

P

padecer del corazón heart
  condition
el padre father
pagar v pay
el pájaro bird
el palacio palace; **~ de las cortes**
  parliament building
los palillos chinos chopsticks
la panadería bakery
los pantalones pants [trousers BE];
  ~ cortos shorts

el pañal diaper [nappy BE]

el pañuelo de paper tissue

el papel paper; ~ **de aluminio** aluminum [kitchen BE] foil; ~ **de cocina** paper towel; ~ **higiénico** toilet paper

el paquete package

para for; ~ **llevar** to go [take away BE]; ~ **no fumadores** non-smoking

el paracetamol acetaminophen [paracetamol BE]

la parada *n* stop; ~ **de autobús** bus stop

el paraguas umbrella

pararse *v* stop

el párking parking garage

el parque playpen; ~ park; ~ **de atracciones** amusement park

el partido game; ~ **de fútbol** soccer [football BE]; ~ **de voleibol** volleyball game

el pasajero passenger; ~ **con billete** ticketed passenger

el pasaporte passport

el pase de acceso a los remontes lift pass

el pasillo aisle

la pasta de dientes toothpaste

la pastelería pastry shop

el patio de recreo playground

el peatón pedestrian

el pecho chest (body part)

el pediatra pediatrician

la pedicura pedicure

pedir *v* order

el peinado hairstyle

el peine comb

la película movie

peligroso dangerous

el pelo hair

el peltre pewter

la peluquería de caballeros barber

la peluquería hair salon

los pendientes earrings

el pene penis

la penicilina penicillin

la pensión bed and breakfast

pequeño small

perder *v* lose (something)

perdido lost

el perfume perfume

el periódico newspaper

la perla pearl

permitir *v* allow, permit

el perro guía guide dog

la persona con discapacidad visual visually impaired person

la picadura de insecto insect bite

picante spicy

picar *v* stamp (a ticket)

el pie foot
la piel skin
la pierna leg
la pieza part (for car)
los pijamas pajamas
la pila battery
la píldora Pill (birth control)
la piscina pool; ~ **cubierta** indoor
  pool; ~ **exterior** outdoor pool;
  ~ **infantil** kiddie [paddling BE]
  pool
la pista trail [piste BE]
la pizzería pizzeria
el placer pleasure
la plancha n iron (clothes)
planchar v iron
la planta floor [storey BE];
  ~ **baja** ground floor
la plata silver;
  ~ **esterlina** sterling silver
el platino platinum
el plato dish (kitchen);
  ~ **principal** main course
la playa beach
la plaza town square
la policía police
la pomada cream (ointment)
ponerse en contacto con v contact
por for; ~ per; ~ **día** per day;
  ~ **favor** please; ~ **hora** per hour;
  ~ **la noche** overnight; ~ **noche**

per night; ~ **semana** per week
el postre dessert
el precio price
precioso beautiful
el prefijo area code
la pregunta question
presentar v introduce
el preservativo condom
la primera clase first class
primero first
los principales sitios de interés
  main attraction
principiante beginner, novice
  (skill level)
la prioridad de paso right of way
la prisa rush
el probador fitting room
probar v taste
el problema problem
el producto good;
  ~ **de limpieza** cleaning product
programar v schedule
prohibir v prohibit
el pronóstico forecast
pronunciar v pronounce
el protector solar sunscreen
provisional temporary
próximo next
el público public
el pueblo village
el puente bridge

la puerta gate (airport); ~ door;
  ~ **de incendios** fire door
el pulmón lung
la pulsera bracelet
el puro cigar

Q

qué what (question)
quedar bien v fit (clothing)
quedarse v stay
la queja complaint
la quemadura solar sunburn
querer v love (someone)
quién who (question)
el quiosco newsstand

R

la ración portion; ~ **para
  niños** children's portion
la rampa para silla de ruedas
  wheelchair ramp
el rap rap (music)
rápido express, fast
la raqueta racket (sports);
  ~ **de nieve** snowshoe
la reacción alérgica
  allergic reaction
recargar v recharge
la recepción reception
la receta prescription
recetar v prescribe

rechazar v decline (credit card)
recibir v receive
el recibo receipt
reciclar recycling
recoger v pick up (something)
la recogida de equipajes
  baggage claim
la recomendación
  recommendation
recomendar v recommend
el recorrido tour; ~ **en autobús**
  bus tour; ~ **turístico** sightseeing
  tour
recto straight
el recuerdo souvenir
el regalo gift
la región region
el registro check-in (hotel);
  ~ **del coche** vehicle registration
la regla period (menstrual)
el Reino Unido United Kingdom
  (U.K.)
la relación relationship
rellenar v fill out (form)
el reloj watch; ~ **de pared** wall
  clock
el remolque trailer
reparar v fix (repair)
el repelente de insectos
  insect repellent
repetir v repeat

la resaca hangover
la reserva reservation;
~ **natural** nature preserve
reservar v reserve
el/la residente de la UE
EU resident
respirar v breathe
el restaurante restaurant
retirar v withdraw; ~ **fondos**
withdrawal (bank)
retrasarse v delay
la reunión meeting
revelar v develop (film)
revisar v check (on something)
la revista magazine
el riñón kidney (body part)
el río river
robado stolen
robar v steal
el robo theft
la rodilla knee
rojo red
romántico romantic
romper v break
la ropa clothing;
~ **interior** underwear
rosa pink
roto broken
el rubgy rugby
la rueda tire [tyre BE];
~ **pinchada** flat tire [tyre BE]

las ruinas ruins
la ruta route; ~ **de**
senderismo walking route

S

la sábana sheet
el sacacorchos corkscrew
el saco de dormir sleeping bag
la sala room; ~ **de conciertos**
concert hall; ~ **de espera**
waiting room; ~ **de reuniones**
meeting room
la salida check-out (hotel)
la salida n exit; ~ **de urgencia**
emergency exit
las salidas departures (airport)
salir v exit, leave
el salón room; ~ **de**
congresos convention hall;
~ **de juegos recreativos** arcade;
~ **de manicura** nail salon
¡Salud! Cheers!
la salud health
las sandalias sandals
sangrar v bleed
la sangre blood
el santuario shrine
la sartén frying pan
la sauna saúna
el secador de pelo hair dryer
la secreción discharge (bodily fluid)

la seda silk
sediento thirsty
la seguridad security
el seguro insurance
seguro safe (protected)
el sello *n* stamp (postage)
el semáforo traffic light
la semana week
semanal weekly
el seminario seminar
el sendero trail; ~ **para bicicletas** bike route
el seno breast
sentarse *v* sit
separado separated (marriage)
ser *v* be
serio serious
el servicio restroom [toilet BE]; ~ service (in a restaurant); ~ **completo** full-service; ~ **de habitaciones** room service; ~ **inalámbrico a internet** wireless internet service; ~ **de internet** internet service; ~ **de lavandería** laundry service; ~ **de limpieza de habitaciones** housekeeping service
la servilleta napkin
sí yes
el sida AIDS

la silla chair; ~ **para niños** child seat; ~ **de ruedas** wheelchair
el símbolo symbol (keyboard)
sin without; ~ **alcohol** non-alcoholic; ~ **grasa** fat free; ~ **receta** over the counter (medication)
la sinagoga synagogue
el sitio de interés attraction (place)
el sobre envelope
el socorrista lifeguard
el sol sun
solamente only
soleado sunny
solo alone
soltero single (marriage)
el sombrero hat
la somnolencia drowsiness
sordo deaf
soso bland
el suavizante conditioner
el subtítulo subtitle
sucio dirty
la sudadera sweatshirt
el suelo floor
el sujetador bra
súper super (fuel)
superior upper
el supermercado grocery store, supermarket

la supervisión supervision
el sur south
el surfista windsurfer

T

la tabla board; **~ de snowboard** snowboard; **~ de surf** surfboard
la talla size; **~ grande** plus size; **~ pequeña** petite size
el taller garage (repair)
el talón de equipaje luggage [baggage BE] ticket
el tampón tampon
la taquilla locker; **~** reservation desk
tarde late (time)
la tarde afternoon
la tarjeta card; **~ de cajero automático** ATM card; **~ de crédito** credit card; **~ de débito** debit card; **~ de embarque** boarding pass; **~ internacional de estudiante** international student card; **~ de memoria** memory card; **~ de negocios** business card; **~ postal** postcard; **~ de seguro** insurance card; **~ de socio** membership card; **~ telefónica** phone card
la tasa fee

el taxi taxi
la taza cup; **~ medidora** measuring cup
el teatro theater; **~ de la ópera** opera house
la tela impermeable groundcloth [groundsheet BE]
el teleférico cable car
el teléfono telephone; **~ móvil** cell [mobile BE] phone; **~ público** pay phone
la telesilla chair lift
el telesquí ski/drag lift
la televisión TV
el templo temple (religious)
temprano early
el tenedor fork
tener *v* have; **~ dolor** *v* hurt (have pain); **~ náuseas** *v* be nauseous
el tenis tennis
la tensión arterial blood pressure
la terminal terminal (airport)
terminar *v* end
la terracotta terracotta
terrible terrible
el texto *n* text (message)
el tiempo time; **~** weather
la tienda store; **~ de alimentos naturales** health food store; **~ de antigüedades** antique store; **~ de bebidas alcohólicas**

liquor store [off-licence BE];
~ **de campaña** tent; ~ **de
deportes** sporting goods store;
~ **de fotografía** camera store;
~ **de juguetes** toy store;
~ **de música** music store;
~ **de recuerdos** souvenir store;
~ **de regalos** gift shop;
~ **de ropa** clothing store
las tijeras scissors
la tintorería dry cleaner
el tipo de cambio exchange rate
tirar *v* pull (door sign)
la tirita bandage
la toalla towel
la toallita baby wipe
el tobillo ankle
el torneo de golf golf
tournament
la torre tower
la tos *n* cough
toser *v* cough
el total total (amount)
trabajar *v* work
tradicional traditional
traducir *v* translate
traer *v* bring
tragar *v* swallow
el traje suit
tranquilo quiet
el tren train; ~ **rápido** express

train
triste sad
la trona highchair
el trozo piece
la tumbona deck chair
el turista tourist

U

último last
la universidad university
uno one
la uña nail; ~ **del
dedo** fingernail;
~ **del pie** toenail
urgente urgent
usar *v* use

V

las vacaciones vacation
[holiday BE]
vaciar *v* empty
la vacuna vaccination
la vagina vagina
la validez valid
valioso valuable
el valle valley
el valor value
el vaquero denim
los vaqueros jeans
el vaso glass (drinking)
el váter químico chemical toilet

vegetariano vegetarian
la vejiga bladder
vender v sell
el veneno poison
venir v come
la ventana window
el ventilador fan (appliance)
ver v see
verde green
el vestido dress (piece of clothing)
el viaje trip
el vidrio glass (material)
viejo old
la viña vineyard
la violación n rape
violar v rape
el visado visa (passport document)
visitar v visit
la vitamina vitamin

la vitrina display case
viudo widowed
vivir v live
vomitar v vomit
el vuelo flight; ~ **internacional** international flight; ~ **nacional** domestic flight

Z

la zapatería shoe store
las zapatillas slippers; ~ **de deporte** sneaker
los zapatos shoes
la zona area; ~ **de compras** shopping area; ~ **de fumadores** smoking area; ~ **para picnic** picnic area
el zoológico zoo
zurcir v mend